D1359123

The Chicago Pragmatists

THE CHICAGO PRAGMATISTS

by Darnell Rucker

UNIVERSITY OF MINNESOTA PRESS · MINNEAPOLIS

Printed in the United States of America at the Lund Press, Minneapolis.
Published in Great Britain, India, and Pakistan by the Oxford University Press, London, Bombay, and Karachi, and in Canada by the Copp Clark Publishing Co. Limited, Toronto.

Library of Congress Catalog Card Number: 69-13188

PREFACE

PHILOSOPHERS in the United States have produced a variety of pragmatisms, beginning with those of Charles S. Peirce and William James. F. C. S. Schiller at Oxford had worked out a pragmatism of his own — which he later called humanism — but that philosophy did not take root in England. Pragmatism remains the one philosophic outlook that is native to the United States.

Also, there have been many schools of philosophy in America, groups of men who shared a concern with the propagation of particular philosophic theories. Some, notably the St. Louis School and the Concord School in the latter part of the nineteenth century, were the creations of strong individuals with missionary spirits. Others were pockets of Scottish commonsensism or German idealism in universities such as Yale, Cornell, Boston, and Johns Hopkins. In each case, however, the philosophizing in these schools was more a defense of some basically European way of thought than a search for a new way.

The founders of pragmatism, Peirce and James, formed no schools. Peirce was effectively excluded from real participation in an academic institution, and he was temperamentally unfitted to be the master of a group of scholars around him. During his short tenure at Johns Hopkins, his lectures on logic did not attract many students, and few of those who did attend understood what he was trying to do. James, on the other hand, from his base in the great Philosophy Department at Harvard, had a wide popular audience for a philosopher. But he also did not attract a stable group of disciples. The presentation of his ideas was a bit too popular for many philosophers of the day, and the department at Harvard was too eclectic for a school to take shape around any one of the members. The swirl of ideas from James, Josiah Royce, George Santayana, Hugo Münsterberg, and George Herbert Palmer was too rapid for a single point of view to solidify as the departmental philosophy.

Only at the new University of Chicago at the turn of the century did there grow up a school of American philosophy. The pragmatism that John Dewey and his colleagues and their students collaborated on there had its roots in James and Peirce, but what emerged from their efforts was distinctively their own and reflected more truly the soil from which it sprang than did either James's or Peirce's thought. Neither James's concern to rescue sentiment from what he saw as the onslaught of science nor Peirce's drive to systematize modern thought represented the main thrust of American culture. The Chicago philosophers shared James's practical orientation, in contrast to Peirce's emphasis on theory; and they accepted Peirce's broad view of the method of science and its application, as opposed to James's fear that science, too narrowly interpreted, was a threat to human values. The Chicago pragmatists saw both science and values arising from human action, and they proceeded to derive an entire philosophy from the analysis of action. This action-derived philosophy turned out to be a pragmatism different from both Peirce's logic-centered thought and James's psychology-based work.

Because the Chicago philosophy reflected an awareness of the interconnections among the advances being made in biology, psychology, and sociology, it was able to provide a method and a perspective for an array of disciplines. And so it was that the Chicago School was a school, not merely in the sense that several men were working together evolving (not just defending) a philosophy, but in the fuller sense that their work had effects in a cluster of fields of thought around philosophy; it was a school with a university full of its progeny. The progeny were as much products of the susceptibility of the new university to untraditional approaches to academic matters as they were of the fecundity of the philosophy. The institutional atmosphere of new beginnings made for an audacity and an experimental spirit in certain areas that could not be expected in more established universities or in more tradition-bound disciplines. Psychology, education, religion, sociology, economics, and political science, for instance, were already in ferment, and at Chicago the Philosophy Department was developing ideas in a form readily relevant to problems in those fields. It is not surprising that the most lasting impact of this thought grounded in human practice has been on the social sciences. The peculiar influences in particular fields were due to special circumstances, of course, but the general structure of the theory was such as to lend itself easily to the sciences of man.

The account given here is of the philosophy constructed by the Chicago group and of the direct impact of that philosophy on other departments in the university. I have attempted to be careful not to attribute any point of view found at Chicago to the influence of the local pragmatism, technically considered, unless I could detect some positive indication that a direct influence had been at work. As I have pointed out further on, the general perspective of pragmatism was widely prevalent in the university and in the country at large during the time that the Chicago School flourished. And I consider the business of tracing the life and influence of ideas in any very specific way to be perilous at best. Therefore I have dealt only with those fields in which I have found acknowledged or obvious links with the Philosophy Department.

One omission requires special explanation. History at Chicago showed none of the overt signs of awareness of pragmatism found in the other social sciences. History, of course, was a humanistic discipline long before there were social sciences; and at Chicago the history faculty retained the prerogative of declaring individual membership in either the Humanities or the Social Sciences Division even when the department was placed under the Social Sciences Division for administrative purposes. History was more traditional from the start than were the newer disciplines in the University. Hermann von Holst was a scholar of repute when he arrived to head the department, and he was just the sort of rock of respectability with which President William Rainey Harper would have liked to staff the whole institution. The mainstays of the History Department—von Holst, Benjamin Terry, James Westfall Thompson, John Franklin Jameson, and Andrew McLaughlin—were hardly men to introduce revolutionary methods of any sort into the writing of history. There were also historians in other departments, George Stephen Goodspeed in comparative religion and James Henry Breasted in oriental languages and literature, for example. But they, too, represented a traditional scholarship in which the inroads of scientific method took a turn different from that in the social sciences proper. (Much the same may be said of the English Department under John Matthews Manly and staffed with such men as Frederick Ives Carpenter, William Vaughn Moody, and Robert Morss Lovett.)

The men with whom this work is concerned were in no sense traditional. They were deliberately breaking with traditions of thought and scholarship, opening new paths, challenging intellectual and academic habits, devising new ideas and terminologies. The very style of writing of many of these people stands in contrast to the more literary tradition of scholarship. There is a brashness, even a crudeness of style that marks their productions as a different breed from the more polished writings of their eastern counterparts. Even so sympathetic a reader as Schiller, in his review of *Studies in Logical Theory*, remarks upon the forbidding style of Dewey and his collaborators in the book. And Dewey did become sensitive to the criticisms of his writing style. But the roughness was a product of hewing out new ways of thinking about the world, and things were developing too rapidly for the men involved to stop to smooth out the exposition of their ideas. In fact, George Herbert Mead was so caught up in rethinking his ideas right to his death that he never took time to set down his philosophy in anything approaching a complete form.

Dewey was the founder and the guiding light of the Chicago School, and his guidance continued long after he had left Chicago to go to Columbia and points abroad. Hence, in the account of the

Chicago philosophy, Dewey's works written both before and after he was at Chicago have been referred to, although the emphasis is upon the writings of the Chicago period. Dewey was a major influence on students in philosophy at Chicago as long as the School lasted. His former colleagues paid careful attention to all that he did, with the result that Chicago students could point to Dewey as their mentor even though they had never encountered him in person.

More people than I can list have been of help to me in the course of this undertaking. The American Council of Learned Societies gave me the opportunity to begin my work, with a fellowship for the year 1960–61. Frederick Eby, Clarence Ayres, and Arthur Murphy (all then at the University of Texas) provided invaluable accounts of the beginning, the middle, and the final periods, respectively, of the Chicago School. Charner Perry, until recently chairman of the Philosophy Department at Chicago, supplied important leads and made available a number of useful items from the Mead papers in the department. The staff of Harper Memorial Library was helpful in my use of the Harper files in the University Archives. Colorado College awarded me a summer grant in 1962 to continue my research, and President Louis T. Benezet helped make the college an exciting and rewarding community of faculty and students. His successor, Lloyd E. Worner, continued that tradition and was kind enough to read and comment on portions of the work as they were completed. Herbert Schneider more than anyone else has continuously supported and encouraged my efforts. Though he is not liable for this book, he was essential to it. And finally my wife, Joy, by her tolerance of my frequent absences in 1960–61, 1962, and 1966 to do research in Chicago and to write in Cripple Creek, Colorado, and by her unfailing confidence in me, made the work possible.

D. R.

CONTENTS

The Chicago Pragmatists

I

INTRODUCTION · *The Men and the University*

THE University of Chicago emerged full blown out of the marshes on the south side of Chicago in 1892. By the time the university celebrated its decennial year, it had won widespread (if sometimes grudging) recognition as one of the leading research institutions in the world, and within its walls were being developed theories whose impact was felt in both the academic and the outside worlds. Among the major enterprises that so quickly made the reputation of the young university was the school of philosophy that was founded there two years after the university opened.

With characteristic generosity, William James proclaimed the advent of the Chicago School in both private and public communications. He expressed a genuine personal pleasure at what was going on at Chicago in a letter written on October 29, 1903: "Chicago University has during the past six months given birth to the fruit of its ten years of gestation under John Dewey. The result is wonderful — a *real school*, and *real Thought*. Important thought, too! Did you ever hear of such a city or such a University? Here [at Harvard] we have thought, but no school. At Yale a school but no thought. Chicago has both." [1] And he made his approval public in a review of *Studies in Logical Theory*, in which he made the name "The Chicago School" official in the philosophic world: "Professor John Dewey, and at least ten of his disciples, have collectively put into the world a statement, homogeneous in spite of so many cooperating minds, of a view of the world, both theoretical and practical, which is so simple, massive, and positive that, in spite of the fact that many parts of it yet need to be worked out, it deserves the title of a new system of philosophy." [2]

The School James recognized had begun to take form in 1894, when Dewey went to Chicago from the University of Michigan and became head professor of philosophy in the two-year-old university on the Midway Plaisance. Dewey brought with him George Herbert Mead, also from Michigan, as assistant professor of philosophy and James Rowland Angell, from the University of Minnesota, as assistant professor of experimental psychology. James Hayden Tufts had come to Chicago in 1892 from Dewey's department at Michigan. Tufts's letter to President William Rainey Harper recommending Dewey for the position of head of the Philosophy Department was one of the decisive factors in Dewey's appointment. Along with Tufts, Charles A. Strong had come to Chicago as associate professor of psychology in the Philosophy Department, but he went to Columbia in 1895. Dewey, Mead, Angell, and Tufts were the nucleus of the Chicago School in the decade from 1894 to 1904, when the foundations of the new philosophy were being laid. Edward Scribner Ames received the first Ph.D. in the Department of Philosophy in 1895 and later joined its staff, applying to religion the principles being developed there. Addison Webster Moore came to Chicago from Cornell in 1894 to study with Dewey and remained to become one of the central figures of the group. Among the graduate students who played a more passing part in the movement were Myron L. Ashley, Kate Gordon, Willard C. Gore, Simon F. McLennan, Arthur K. Rogers, Amy Tanner, Helen Bradford Thompson, and Henry W. Stuart.

Shortly after Dewey arrived, the Department of Pedagogy was formed with Dewey at its head, so that in effect philosophy, psychology, and education were united under one man. The name of the Department of Pedagogy was later changed to the Department of Education, and in 1902 Dewey was named director of the School of Education, when the Chicago Institute, the Chicago Manual

Training School, and the University Elementary School were merged with the Department of Education. From 1896, the psychological and logical theories being developed in the laboratory and classrooms of the Philosophy Department were applied to learning situations in the University Elementary School, with the aid of Dewey's wife, Alice Chipman Dewey, and Mrs. Ella Flagg Young, later superintendent of schools in Chicago.

The Chicago philosophy was, of course, a form of pragmatism. It is closer to James's pragmatism than to that of Charles S. Peirce in its belief in the practical nature of all knowledge. But it is perhaps closer to Peirce in its conception and use of the method of science. The psychology identified with Chicago is called "functionalism," and Dewey later named his logic "instrumentalism." Functionalism came to be peculiarly attached to Angell and Harvey Carr in Chicago's Psychology Department after it separated from Philosophy. "Pragmatism" was long a polemical term in philosophy and still is in many quarters. James's use of such phrases as "cash value," "expedience," and "that which *pays*" in his theory of truth laid pragmatism open to considerable scholarly vituperation — to the extent that Peirce, who coined the term "pragmatism," renounced it in favor of "pragmaticism" in the hope that the philosophical jousters would leave the latter term alone. And Dewey appears to have had James's "The Will to Believe" in mind when he stated the following disclaimer: "This theory may be called pragmatism. But it is a type of pragmatism quite free from dependence upon a voluntaristic psychology. It is not complicated by reference to emotional satisfactions or the play of desires." [3] To many people pragmatism still means a short-sighted, expediential view of the world and of knowledge. But for good or ill, it remains the aptest designation for the Chicago brand of thought, and like other names it has to take its chances on misinterpretations, both ignorant and willful.

The central concept in the Chicago philosophy is that of activity. Activity is at once biological, psychological, and ethical. It is directly connected to the biological concept of function, the notion of organic process; it involves the idea of an agent with a feeling, emotive, willing nature; and it implies an object or purpose toward which movement is directed. But in this view of concrete activity, biological function is not mere mechanical process, nor is the agent a supernatural spiritual being, nor the end any kind of absolute. Function involves growth, agents are natural elements of natural processes, and ends are always tentative, changing as activity progresses.

The world view that emerges from such a concern with activity has three important features. First, it is a process theory: activity is something going on, and agents or persons and objects or the world are alike results of the process. Second, agents are essentially social beings: consciousness is the product of processes in which a number of agents interact. And third, ends are relative to the conditions of activity at a given time: a genuine evolutionary process is one in which real novelty enters, invalidating preconceived, fixed goals of action.

The University of Chicago provided a unique environment for the growth of such a view, a thoroughly American philosophy. All the elements of activity that any pragmatist could ever wish for were much in evidence in this developing university and in this huge city just feeling its power and possibilities. Under President Harper and a dedicated board of trustees, the University of Chicago was making astounding progress in building a college, a graduate school, and various professional schools. In addition to the sums John D. Rockefeller was pouring into the project ($35,000,000 by 1910), large amounts of money were coming from Chicagoans. In 1892, to meet the conditions of a gift from Marshall Field, the university raised more than a million dollars in ninety days in Chicago alone. At the end of ten years, fourteen major buildings were completed and six were under construction on a site that had been considered a hopeless marsh in 1892.

When the university officially opened its doors in the fall of 1892, Harper had a staff of 120, including such luminaries as Thomas C. Chamberlin and Rollin D. Salisbury in geology, William G. Hale in Latin, Harry Pratt Judson in political science, J. Laurence Laughlin in political economy, Albert A. Michelson in physics, Albion W. Small in sociology, Paul Shorey in Greek, John U. Nef in chemistry, Hermann von Holst and Benjamin Terry in history, Henry H. Donaldson in neurology, Eliakim H. Moore and Oskar Bolza in mathematics, Jacques Loeb in physiology, Charles O. Whitman in biology, Carl D. Buck in Sanscrit, Frank B. Tarbell in classical archaeology, and Ernest D. Burton in New Testament literature. On this first faculty were the former presidents of eight colleges and universities,* fifteen of the ablest scientists in the nation from Clark University, a large portion of Yale's Department of Semitic Languages, and other individual scholars from Brown, Bryn Mawr, Cornell, Freiburg, Illinois, Michigan, Minnesota, Northwestern, Wisconsin, and Yale – all obtained before a single permanent building had been completed.

These established scholars did not come to Chicago because of the relatively high salaries alone. Many of them came because Harper promised them more freedom in developing their departments and their researches than they could find in older institutions. Albion Small, for instance, left Colby to found the first graduate Department of Sociology in the world. Dewey came two years later despite what he considered an inadequate salary because Chicago offered to let him work in psychology and education, as well as philosophy, an opportunity that he could not expect at Michigan.

Harper was breaking many of the most revered traditions of the academic community in his organization of the university. He stated his views on the experimental nature of his institution at the third convocation, in June 1893:

Until the founding of Johns Hopkins University, there was but one type of college in America. No institution doing real university work existed. With the establishment of the University of Chicago another type, it is believed, has been introduced, differing essentially from the college of historic character, and, just as essentially,

* Galusha Anderson of Denison University, Thomas C. Chamberlin of the University of Wisconsin, Howard B. Grose of the University of South Dakota, Franklin Johnson of Ottawa University, George W. Northrup of Baptist Union Theological Seminary, Alice Freeman Palmer of Wellesley College, Ezekial G. Robinson of Brown University, and Albion W. Small of Colby University.

from the type of the Johns Hopkins. That a century or more should have passed with no effort other than to duplicate efforts already made, is difficult to understand. The field for experiment in educational work is as vast as any that may present itself in other departments of activity. If only those who experiment will be quick to discard that which shows itself to be wrong, the cause of education has nothing to fear from experiment.[4]

Harper made the University Press and University Extension integral parts of the university. Instruction was organized into four quarters of twelve weeks each, so that the university was operating on full schedule for the entire year. This innovation altered the time-honored semester system with its summer break, and it did away with the tradition of college classes identified by a common graduation year. A student could complete his requirements and graduate in any of the four quarters. Courses were classified as majors or minors; a major required two hours of classwork a day four or five times a week and a minor one hour a day. A student was supposed to take one major and one minor at a time, for either a six- or a twelve-week period, the purpose being to increase concentration in a given subject and to avoid what Harper called the "surface treatment" necessitated by a student's being involved in six to eight different courses at once. Instead of the usual four-year curriculum, there was a Junior College for broad, general work and a Senior College for beginning preparation for graduate and professional work. And Harper added what he called University Affiliations, a system whereby Chicago was to be associated with other colleges and universities to permit exchange of faculty, students, and ideas.

Most of these schemes were not original with Harper, but the total plan was new—and rather startling in academic circles. Not all of the original system persisted. The idea of affiliations was dropped rather early, although Chicago has cooperated with other institutions throughout its history on a less formal basis. The terms "major" and "minor" were later done away with, but the idea of concentrated work in a few courses at a time has been continued in both the college and the graduate schools. The quarter plan has been a success, as have the Press and the extension work in University College and home-study courses.

Thus the University of Chicago provided an atmosphere of energy and of breaking with the past that was well suited to the development of American traditions of thought distinct from a European heritage. The city of Chicago, too, contributed to this atmosphere. New paths were being marked out in Chicago in education, social work, and philanthropy before the university was founded. Francis W. Parker had attracted worldwide attention with his educational practices at the Cook County Normal School * from 1883 on. Jane Addams had founded Hull House in 1889, and Dewey had been one of the lecturers there while he was still at Michigan. And in 1891, William Kent, a young Chicago millionaire, had started clearance of slum and red-light property he owned and construction of a playground for children in the poor neighborhood. Charles R. Crane was also setting an example in philanthropy at the time. Both these men were to become mainstays of Dewey's experimental school at the university.

The University of Chicago quickly became an important part of the social ferment in Chicago. The University of Chicago Settlement took its place in the stockyards district in 1894 to work along with Hull House. President Harper served on the Chicago Board of Education, and a large number of his faculty were actively engaged in work with the elementary and secondary schools of Chicago and other sections of Illinois. The faculty also provided members and chairmen for a wide range of organizations and commissions concerned with philanthropy, improved sanitation, slum clearance, cultural developments, waterways, labor legislation, strike settlements, and a host of other activities. Such practical endeavors were encouraged as fitting for a university, providing a broad field for testing ideas and theories.† In fact Harper defended

* The Normal School later became the Chicago Institute which merged with the university in 1901. Parker died shortly after the merger.

† Several attempts were made to establish an engineering or other technical school in the university, but they all failed. See Richard J. Storr, *Harper's University: The Beginnings* (Chicago: University of Chicago Press, 1966), pp. 133–35, 285–86.

the emphasis upon pure science in the university by pointing out that "sooner or later in an environment like that of Chicago the practical side would be sufficiently cared for." [5] Therefore the university was immediately concerned with intellectual inquiry into all sorts of problems, while the city around it provided a vast laboratory for testing solutions.

In a sense, however, the university's development as a great scientific research center and as the home of a new empiricism in philosophy was accidental. Tufts reported [6] that Harper had told him in January 1891 that he intended to build three especially strong departments, Semitics, classics, and philosophy. It was only when financial troubles at Clark University made a large number of scientists available that Harper revised his intent and began to make the sciences a central consideration. Moreover, Harper had tried to get George Herbert Palmer, Jacob Gould Schurman, and E. Benjamin Andrews to head the Department of Philosophy. They were established, solidly respectable men. But they turned his offers down,* and upon Tufts's recommendation, Harper offered the post to Dewey.† It is significant that Tufts said of Dewey: "He is a man of religious nature, is a church-member and believes in working with the churches." [7] This description hardly fits the Dewey who came to Chicago – or Mead or Moore either, for that

* It is interesting to note that Palmer gave the following reason for refusing Harper's offer after lengthy correspondence: "I cannot feel that your University can ever escape its sectarian entanglements and come into assured power." (Letter from Palmer to Harper, dated April 2, 1892, in the Archives of the University of Chicago.) Palmer's wife, Alice Freeman Palmer, did accept an appointment at Chicago as dean of women.

† William James had recommended Charles S. Peirce to Harper for the Chicago Philosophy Department. James's letter has not been found, so far as I know, but there is a letter from George H. Palmer of Harvard to Harper, dated June 4, 1892, in the University of Chicago Archives referring to James's recommendation. Palmer says in the letter: "I am astonished at James' recommendation of Peirce. Of course my impressions may be erroneous, and I have no personal acquaintance with Peirce. I know, too, very well his eminence as a logician. But from so many sources I have heard of his broken and dissolute character that I should advise you to make most careful inquiries before engaging him. I am sure it is suspicions of this sort which have prevented his appointment here, and I suppose the same causes procured his dismissal from Johns Hopkins." This was enough for Harper to dismiss consideration of Peirce.

matter. In view of Harper's religious background and the religious emphasis in the Baptist-founded university, it seems doubtful to say the least that Harper would have hired Dewey had he known the line that Dewey's thought was taking.*

In light of its later history, it is interesting to recall that the University of Chicago was founded by the American Baptist Education Society to be a national university for Baptists, following upon the failure of the old University of Chicago and of Columbian University in Washington, D.C.† At the start, the society adopted a policy "to exercise no control over the financial affairs of the institution beyond the time when, in the judgment of the Board, the institution is solidly founded." [8] And the university was given financial autonomy as soon as sufficient funds were secured. Moreover, religious tests or requirements were explicitly excluded for faculty or students. The original resolution of the society did provide that the president and two-thirds of the trustees should always be members of Baptist churches. This requirement was later dropped, and the Baptists gave up all formal control of the university in 1931.

Harper can probably be credited with protecting the university from undue religious interference. At the dedication of a bas-relief portrait of Harper in 1931, J. M. Powis Smith, who had been Harper's literary secretary and was professor of Semitic languages and

* Differences on religion have been mentioned among the causes of the rift between Harper and Dewey that led to Dewey's leaving Chicago in 1904. Mrs. Katherine C. Mayhew and Mrs. Anna C. Edwards, in their book *The Dewey School* (New York: D. Appleton-Century, 1936), say that Dewey resigned over what he considered a breach of faith by Harper when Dewey's elementary school was incorporated in the School of Education. The facts remain hidden, the letters of resignation of Dewey and his wife being missing from the Chicago Archives. Robert L. McCaul has given an account of Dewey's last days at Chicago in *School and Society*, 89 (no. 2191): 202–6 (April 22, 1961). There is also an account in Storr, *Harper's University*, pp. 296–302, of some of Dewey's problems with the elementary school.

† The old University of Chicago was founded in 1857, largely through the offices of Stephen A. Douglas, and after constant financial struggles, closed in 1886 when an insurance company foreclosed its mortgage on the university's one building. The board of trustees later relinquished its right to the name University of Chicago so the new Baptist institution could be so called. Columbian University changed its name to George Washington University in 1904 and passed from Baptist control.

literature, pointed out that Harper had placed the Department of Semitic Languages and Literature in the Graduate School instead of in the Divinity School where it belonged because the Divinity School had its own board composed of very conservative Baptists who were likely to make trouble for any staff member departing from traditional Old Testament interpretations, and Harper wanted his Old Testament scholars to be as free as possible from outside attack.[9]

On the other hand, Harper brought the first student of religion into the Department of Philosophy. Edward Scribner Ames had been a student in the Divinity School and the Philosophy Department at Yale. He relates that he was offered a fellowship in philosophy by Harper, whom Ames had met through his uncle, Sanford Scribner, a trustee of the University of Chicago Divinity School. Ames went to Chicago in 1894 and finished his dissertation begun at Yale, "The History of Agnosticism," the following year. When Harper wanted to keep Ames as an instructor in philosophy, Dewey protested that the department needed an instructor in experimental psychology.[10] According to Ames, Harper did try to offer him a post anyway, but Ames had already accepted a position at Butler College.[11] Harper was instrumental in bringing Ames back to Chicago for the summer quarter of 1900 and eventually in getting him a part-time appointment in the Department of Philosophy.

Needless to say, the Chicago School was considerably more interested in science than religion, and the new concepts of religion that later developed in connection with the School were a far cry from the Baptist theology of the university's founders. Ames became the minister of the Hyde Park Church of the Disciples of Christ in 1900, and there, adjacent to the University of Chicago campus, he put into practice the liberal religious ideas he was developing in his classes a few blocks away.

At any rate, although it was founded by a conservative religious organization, Chicago rapidly became a hub of scientific activity, and the Chicago pragmatism spread its influence throughout the university. Perhaps the most important single instrument for the dissemination of ideas from the Philosophy Department in the beginning was the University Elementary School, or the Laboratory School, as it came to be known. Scholars from all over the university came to teach and observe there, and interest in the educational theories being evolved led many of them to an acquaintance with the new philosophy. Thomas Chamberlin talked to the children about his new planetesimal theory of the origin of the solar system, John M. Coulter planned and guided experiments on plant relations, and Charles O. Whitman in zoology, Jacques Loeb in physiology, William I. Thomas, George Vincent, and Albion Small in sociology, Frederick Starr in anthropology, Rollin D. Salisbury in geography, Albert Michelson in physics, Alexander Smith in chemistry, and Henry C. Cowles in ecology also cooperated in the school program. Mead, Tufts, and Angell were directly involved in the planning and teaching experiments until Dewey left Chicago.[12] Few experiments have enlisted so many eminent men from so many different fields as did this Laboratory School, and few new philosophies have had such a rich testing ground for their ideas as did the Chicago brand of pragmatism.

The labors of the philosophers and psychologists had their parallels and their influences in other departments of the university, especially in sociology, religion, and economics. In sociology, Small was impressed by Dewey's educational and social theories; and William I. Thomas, Robert E. Park, and Ellsworth Faris, among others, found the experimental approach of Dewey and Mead useful in their sociological studies. The religious psychology of Ames and the critical approach to the study of the Bible that Harper fostered worked to produce one of the main trends in what is called liberal religion. Thorstein Veblen, of course, was scandalizing economists with his unorthodox ideas, which in part bear strong resemblance to those of the Chicago School. Wesley C. Mitchell's institutional economics shows the effects of his seven years at Chicago, where he worked with Veblen and the Philosophy Department; and Clarence Ayres later made a direct application of pragmatism to economics.

But the closest ties in this intellectual milieu for some time remained those among philosophy, psychology, and education, even after these disciplines were separated into three distinct departments. Graduate students in each of the fields continued to move about freely in all three areas, and the philosophy faculty continued to teach in education and psychology. Mead was listed in the Department of Education until 1911 and Tufts until 1915. Ames taught courses in the Department of Psychology until 1924 and Mead until 1926. Tufts served briefly as acting chairman of the Department of Psychology when Angell resigned in 1920 to become president of the Carnegie Corporation. The actual interchange of ideas that gave such vigor to all the areas touched upon by the Chicago School was at its peak during the decade 1894–1904, however, and this was the golden era of the School.

A widespread sense of related endeavor uncommon to academic life pervaded the university during that period. Scholars not only were aware of what their colleagues were doing but took account in their own work of the contributions of their colleagues, as is evidenced by the cross-references in the voluminous writings of the early faculty. The graduate students caught this spirit of community, too, and they were made to feel a part of the creative activity going on around them. And as their publications warrant, they were a part of it.

In all probability, part of the solidarity of the early Chicago faculty was caused by the reactions of segments of the academic world to this brash young institution. For example, one easterner, who had entertained hopes that Rockefeller would finance a new university in New York City, exclaimed that Chicago was about as likely a place for a great university as the Fiji Islands. Marion Talbot, long-time dean of women and professor of household science at Chicago, reported something of the same attitude on the part of her friends when she departed from Boston. "On September 19, 1892, Alice Freeman Palmer, William Gardner Hale, and I left Boston for Chicago. As we boarded the train at the South Station a friend of mine pressed into my hand a little box. 'It holds,' she said, 'a fragment of Plymouth Rock.' This was symbolic of the attitude of our Boston friends toward the new educational venture in Chicago. It was something built on the sands. The academic system with which Boston was familiar was founded upon a rock."[13] Other critics were even less kind, as Shailer Mathews, dean of the Divinity School, recalled some years later: "I remember that one of the leading journals of the East, with that fine spirit of detachment from the American spirit that characterizes the outposts of European culture of the Atlantic Coast, prophesied that soon the output of doctors of philosophy in the University of Chicago would rival the output of pigs in the Stock Yards. The most familiar form of humor, however, was to refer to our institution as a continuation of the Midway shows, or 'Harper's Three-Ring Circus.' "[14]

Harper himself was warned against leaving the safe confines of Yale for the unknown wilds of Chicago. Professor George T. Ladd of Yale's Philosophy Department wrote to Harper: "You would in my judgment make the great and irreparable mistake of your life. . . . You 'draw' well, undoubtedly. But, my dear fellow, back of you and of all of us here is the one great power that lends to us more effectiveness than we contribute to it. It is 'Yale' that draws. While you are in your prime few men will care for a Ph.D. or even a B.A. from your new university, who can manage to get a similar degree from an institution like this."[15] President Timothy Dwight, however, reacted to Harper's impending move more with injured asperity than with admonition: "I owe it to myself, however, and to you, to say to you frankly that, in my judgment, after all that has been done for you at Yale, and all that I have myself done, to secure your position, you cannot honorably leave your Yale professorship for this place at Chicago." And, later, "In this case of yours I have been, in a peculiar degree, the beginning, middle, and end of the movement which has secured your position at Yale by a permanent endowment. . . . I would much rather you had never come to Yale at all, than to have you remain until this effort had been undertaken and completed and then leave for a new position."[16]

After Harper did undertake the Chicago job, there were many who resented his tactics in establishing the university. Probably the most bitter resentment was that of G. Stanley Hall, president of

Clark University. Twenty-one years after the event, Hall still felt a strong sense of injury in recalling Harper's raid on his institution:

Very soon after this, President Harper of the University of Chicago appeared upon the scene. He had made many proposals to eminent men to join his staff but they had been turned down because of a critical attitude toward a "Standard-Oil institution," a very grave obstacle at that time to that very able and sagacious organizer but which has long since been forgotten in the splendid work the institution has accomplished. Dr. Harper, learning of the dissatisfaction here, had at Professor Whitman's house met and engaged one morning the majority of our staff, his intentions and even his presence being unknown to me. Those to whom we paid $4,000, he gave $7,000; to those we paid $2,000, he offered $4,000, etc., taking even instructors, docents, and fellows. This proved really to be the nucleus and, I think, the turning point in the early critical stage of the development of the Chicago institution.

When this was done he called on me, inviting me also to join the hegira at a salary larger than I was receiving – which of course I refused – and then told me what he had done. I replied that it was an act of wreckage for us comparable to anything that the worst trust had ever attempted against its competitors but he asked, "What could I do?" recounting the above difficulties he had had in gathering a staff. I finally told him that if he would revise his list, releasing a few of our men and taking one or two others whom he had omitted, I would bear the calamity silently and with what grace I could, although I felt his act comparable to that of a housekeeper who would steal in at the back door to engage servants at a higher price. To this he demurred, and I finally threatened, unless he would make such few revisions of his list as I suggested, to make a formal appeal to the public and to Mr. Rockefeller himself to see if this trust magnate (who was at that time about at the height of his unpopularity and censure and who was said to have driven many smaller competing firms out of existence by slow strangling methods of competition) would justify such an assassination of an institution as had that day been attempted here (for Harper had made advances to nearly all of our staff, even those who remained loyal, and was evidently ready to make a clean sweep). He finally assented, even taking at least one man here who covered the exact field of another he had previously engaged and canceling his engagements with one or two of the younger men I particularly wanted, although to my surprise and regret he felt himself justified in informing those whose status was changed by this revision that it was at my direction.

I had spent much time, travel, and effort in gathering this very distinguished group of men, and I told him that his action was like that of the eagle who robbed the fishhawk of his prey.[17]

Further criticisms of Harper and the university were occasioned by the scandal that arose upon the firing of Edward W. Bemis, an associate professor of political economy in the Extension Department, in 1895. Several eastern newspapers gave quite a play to the story, one of them quoting champions of Bemis to the effect that he had been fired at the instigation of Charles Yerkes, "the notorious person whom common fame in Chicago credits with having done more than all other men combined to corrupt the municipal politics of that city, by systematic bribery in the interest of street railway corporations." [18] Yerkes was an early benefactor of the university and at the time of the Bemis incident was involved in a street railway franchise fight with the city of Chicago. Albion Small published in the *American Journal of Sociology*, which he edited, the following as "a fair specimen of numerous communications which have come to hand during the past month":

Dear Sir: I have just received your interesting circular. I have the highest respect for the able members of the University faculty who are at the head of the undertaking and for the scholars who are cooperating with them. But I feel it a duty to say that I can look for no lasting good from a work that is conducted by an educational institution founded by the arch-robber of America and which already, by its treatment of Professor Bemis, exhibits a determination to throttle free investigation of sociological or economic subjects wherever there is any danger of running counter to plutocratic interests. For this reason I regard the tendency to make our higher educational institutions in this country dependent upon private benefactions a very serious menace to the cause of scientific truth, and calculated to make our scholars timorous and truculent, rather than fearlessly devoted to arriving at the truth, pure and simple, as science demands.[19]

Small followed the letter with an editorial defending the freedom both of the university faculty and of the pages of his journal; and, later, statements by Harper, Small, and Nathaniel Butler of the

Extension Department were circulated in answer to the charges against the university. In fact, Harper seems to have been concerned with establishing the freedom of his faculty,* and he made a very strong statement about coercion of faculty in his *President's Report* for 1892–1902. Rockefeller himself took pains to make known his own hands-off policy with regard to the entire management of the university.[20] But doubts about the chastity of the university persisted, in spite of all denials. When Veblen wrote Lester Ward that he would like to leave Chicago, Ward wrote to a friend: "I heard that Veblen was likely to have to leave the University. They will all have to go ultimately who are above the wretched chauvinism that is required and expected." [21]

All but the most obdurate critics were at least partially chastened, however, by the rapidity with which Chicago established itself as a center of scholarship in many fields. In addition to the men already mentioned, the Chicago faculty during the first ten years included Charles E. Merriam in political science; John F. Jameson and James Westfall Thompson in history; James Henry Breasted in Egyptology; Edgar J. Goodspeed in Biblical Greek; John Matthews Manly, Robert Herrick, Robert Morss Lovett, and Frederick Ives Carpenter in English; Julius Stieglitz in chemistry; Herbert J. Davenport in economics; James Parker Hall and Ernst Freund in law; Clyde W. Votaw in New Testament literature; Leonard E. Dickson in mathematics; Robert A. Millikan in physics; Frank R. Lillie in zoology; and Harry G. Wells and Howard T. Ricketts in pathology.

Of the men in the Philosophy Department, Dewey established the widest reputation and exercised the greatest influence. He supplied the original direction for the new philosophy, whether psychology or logic is viewed as the base from which it was developed.

* Harper's stand on academic freedom was ambiguous, however – as were many of his statements to the faculty. For instance, he felt it proper to admonish professors for public expressions which might antagonize segments of the business world. See Richard Hofstadter and Walter P. Metzger, *The Development of Academic Freedom in the United States* (New York: Columbia University Press, 1955), pp. 427–36; see also Storr, *Harper's University*, pp. 96–99.

Dewey's seminar in logic at the university was one of the most important single elements in the establishment of the School, and *Studies in Logical Theory*, which resulted from this seminar, first set forth the cooperative nature of the early movement. Dewey was the master of the Chicago School, although far from the stereotype of a master. The other men in the department did not sit at his feet and go forth to expound his doctrines (despite James's use of the term "disciples" in the quotation cited earlier). Moore is the only one of the group who was a student of Dewey's, and all of them seemed to move independently from a common point of view. But this point of view was generally adhered to without any serious disagreement from the time the group first began to work as a department. Arthur E. Murphy told me of his discussion of Dewey's *The Quest for Certainty* with Mead, in the course of which he asked Mead if he really believed what Dewey said in that book. Mead, Murphy said, drew himself up and replied, "Every word!"

Angell moved away from the center of the group when a separate Department of Psychology was set up in 1905. Ames's attention was focused to a large extent on his Hyde Park Church, although his writings on religion constitute an interesting facet of the Chicago philosophy. And Dewey's direct personal leadership ended when he went to Columbia in 1905. Mead, Moore, Ames, and Tufts, however, remained at Chicago until their respective retirements, maintaining the Chicago School almost until the very end. It was only as their retirements drew near that they began to add other philosophic viewpoints to the department.

"Quiet," "shy," and "unassuming" are the terms used to describe Dewey, but he must have been, at the same time, firm and determined in order to accomplish what he did during his ten years at Chicago, particularly in establishing and financing hs experimental school. Harper sometimes gave him little help or encouragement in that quarter.[22] Dewey's steady stream of publications rapidly gained him a pre-eminent position in the philosophical world. He was usually in the forefront of whatever was going on in the world of ideas, restating his fundamental concepts in whatever new ways were necessary to combat the new realism, formalism in logic, positivism in ethics, or whatever else was at the center of the stage in opposition to his instrumentalism. And Dewey ranged wider and farther in his writings than did any of the others of the Chicago group, producing, after he left Chicago, significant volumes in logic, ethics, aesthetics, politics, social psychology, educational theory, and philosophy of nature.

Less well known than Dewey, Mead did not travel as far afield in his interests, nor did he have anything like the influence Dewey has had upon the intellectual and practical world of his time. But in those areas of primary interest to him, Mead was a profound thinker, digging deep for the solid philosophic ground of his ideas. All along the line in the development of the Chicago philosophy, Mead makes distinctions clear and bases firm in whatever he discusses. His social psychology, his theory of action, and his philosophy of nature were important contributions to the new empiricism. Unfortunately, he published little of the results of his work, although his colleagues and students have published four important volumes from his manuscripts and student notes: *The Philosophy of the Present*, *Mind, Self and Society*, *Movements of Thought in the Nineteenth Century*, and *The Philosophy of the Act*.[23] Dewey said of Mead: "For him philosophy was less acquired from without, a more genuine development from within, than in the case of any thinker I have known. . . . I dislike to think what my own thinking might have been were it not for the seminal ideas which I derived from him. For his ideas were always genuinely original; they started one thinking in directions where it had never occurred to one that it was worth while even to look." [24]

This very originality made language for expressing his ideas a difficulty. Again in Dewey's words, "If he had borrowed his ideas from without, he could have borrowed his language from the same source." [25] And while Dewey considered Mead most valuable in philosophic discussion, others outside the circle of the School thought him uncommunicative and forbidding. Mead always had a devoted band of followers, but he remained a self-contained mystery to many.

His classroom style, famous with many generations of students in the Philosophy Department at Chicago, contributed to his reputation as a remote, unapproachable scholar. His classes, as a former student reported, were usually large, and he would not appear until everyone had been seated for some minutes, whereupon he would stride to the front of the room, sit down, take up a piece of chalk or other object, fix his eyes on a corner of the ceiling, and begin talking without any sign of awareness that there was anyone else present. He would cogitate aloud without interruption for the duration of the hour; then just before the time was up, without stopping his lecture, he would walk to the back of the room, stop talking precisely at the end of the hour, dart out the door, shutting it behind him. Before the most agile student could get out of the room, Mead was on his bicycle and off for home. As one student remarked, Professor Mead conversed with God and allowed the students to listen in.

But while he seemed self-contained in the development of his ideas, Mead was far from a recluse. True to his ideas, he was involved in the problems of his community—in the educational, civic, and philanthropic activities in and around Chicago. He was associated with the National Charities and Corrections Conference; he was vice-president of the Immigrants' Protective League of Chicago; he served on a committee of the City Club of Chicago to investigate the needs of the Chicago public school system and was for several years president of the club; he was vice-president of the Public Education Association of Chicago and was an active advocate of the development of vocational education in Chicago and Illinois; he was chairman of a city committee in 1919 for cooperation with city and federal officers in the suppression of vice in Chicago and its environs; he was chairman of the Cook County branch of the League to Enforce Peace in 1919; in World War I, he was named director of war courses in the Student Army Training Corps for Missouri, Kansas, and Colorado; and he was a frequent speaker before civic groups, women's clubs, and labor organizations. Mead also was one of the key figures in the settlement of the famous garment workers' strike in Chicago in 1910–11. He was thus a paradoxical combination of an almost ivory-tower philosopher and an active man of affairs. Perhaps this is why he appeared not to feel the need for other men's ideas: he derived many of his own ideas directly from participation in the life of Chicago, that most practical of cities, in the first quarter of this century.

Dewey's social psychology (as evidenced in *Human Nature and Conduct* and elsewhere) owes much to Mead. But Mead's most important direct influence seems to have been on the sociologists at Chicago. During the twenties the Sociology Department was sometimes called an outpost of George Herbert Mead. William I. Thomas, Ellsworth Faris, Ernest Burgess, Robert Park, and Louis Wirth, among others, showed Mead's influence. The real philosophic appraisal of Mead is yet to come, but there is little doubt of his central importance in the development of the Chicago School.

Tufts is the most difficult of the group to evaluate. He preceded Dewey at Chicago, as has been pointed out, and he was an important figure in the university's growth. He published regularly; he was editor of the *School Review* and of the *International Journal of Ethics* and served on the board of the *Psychological Bulletin*; and he was president of the American Philosophical Association, the Western Philosophical Association, and the Pacific Philosophical Association. And Tufts devoted considerable time to administrative duties in the university. He was appointed chairman of the Department of Philosophy when Dewey left, and he held that post until he retired in 1930. He was dean of the Senior College, 1899–1904 and 1907–8, dean of faculties from 1923 until 1926, and vice-president of the university for educational work from 1924 until 1926.

There was less of the pioneer in Tufts than in the other members of the Philosophy Department. James, for instance, ignored Tufts's article in *The Decennial Publications of the University of Chicago* when he reviewed the work of the Chicago School. That article, "On the Genesis of the Aesthetic Categories,"[26] related aesthetics to social psychology. Its thesis, however, was developed in the language and manner of sociology and it seemed on the surface to bear little relation to the groundbreaking work of Dewey, Mead, Moore, and Angell in the same volume. Tufts's previous article

"Can Epistemology Be Based on Mental States?"[27] is one of the important early presentations of the fundamental point of view of the Chicago School that subject and object in knowledge are abstractions, not metaphysical realities; and some of his writings in ethics have been important as an approach to a pragmatic moral theory.[28] But his part of Dewey and Tuft's *Ethics*[29] and many of his other publications were more sociological-historical than philosophical in tone.

Tufts also was more observant of the formal religious elements of the university than were Dewey, Mead, and Moore. The first indication of this concern was his letter to Harper about Dewey quoted above (page 10). He served as the university preacher on several occasions, and while the term "preacher" was very broadly interpreted at Chicago, this role does imply a greater deference to the organized religious segment of the university than Dewey, Mead, or Moore showed. Tufts served several times as a representative of the university at meetings of the Religious Education Association, which had been one of Harper's pet projects. At the first meeting of this association, when Dewey was asked for the first and last time to address the gathering, he told the assemblage that religious education should be based on systematic study of child psychology in the same way as any other kind of education, rather than on adult religious conceptions.[30]

Tufts, like Mead, was active in the civic affairs of Chicago. He was appointed chairman of the Illinois Committee on Social Legislation in 1913; he was director of war courses in the Student Army Training Corps for Illinois, Wisconsin, and Michigan during World War I; he served as chairman of the Board of Arbitration in the Hart, Schaffner, and Marx clothing industry; and he was chairman of a committee to solicit funds for unemployment relief in 1931. He did not, however, translate his practical experience into theoretical ideas as Mead did. As a consequence, while he was applying pragmatic principles to various problems, he did not further the philosophic development of those ideas to the extent that some of his colleagues did.

Moore, on the other hand, devoted almost all his time to dealing with ideas instead of with community matters. He made notable contributions to the logical theory developed in the early period of the School, and he took over Dewey's logic course when Dewey went to Columbia. Matilde Castro Tufts,* in a talk at memorial services for Moore, said that she had been a student in the logic course when it changed hands.[31] The students had been apprehensive over the change, but, she reported, their fears were shortly put to rest and they found that Moore helped them see more clearly many of the things Dewey had previously talked about. Mrs. Tufts's remarks seem an appropriate characterization of much of Moore's career. His logic and metaphysics courses became central for most of the students passing through the Department of Philosophy, and he was the unofficial spokesman for the Chicago School in the philosophy journals, taking on all comers who criticized the Chicago position. An able polemicist, he could restate, expand, and clarify a point of view (he did this especially with reference to logic) with great verbal skill. But little that he wrote after some of his logic papers in the first decade gave rise to new ideas or even new developments of old ideas. Logic remained to the end his primary interest – the instrumental logic of *Studies in Logical Theory* – and he never came to grips with the rise of formal logic that eclipsed instrumental logic in the twenties and thirties. Since formal logic has had an almost complete triumph, Moore has dropped from sight in the philosophic world. He is seldom mentioned any more, but for a time he was a leader in the spread of the ideas of the new pragmatism and did yeoman service in making the rest of the intellectual world pay attention to what was going on at Chicago. Mead said of Moore that he "became in the philosophic world after Mr. Dewey the most important and most authoritative member of the so-called Chicago school." [32]

Ames's work as a graduate student at Chicago was with Tufts and Mead. He recalls that his first encounter with Dewey was in his Ph.D. oral examination.[33] But Ames credits Tufts, Mead, Moore, and Dewey with reshaping his thinking. He was continuously in-

* James H. Tufts married Matilde Castro in 1923, following the death of his first wife in 1920.

volved in the work of the Disciples Divinity House at the university from the time of his arrival in Chicago: helping to raise money for its first building; teaching courses; editing *The Scroll*, the publication of the Campbell Institute of the Disciples; and serving as dean from 1927 to 1945. In the Hyde Park Church he preached and applied his philosophy and psychology of religion and gathered about him a fiercely devoted congregation. Ames was a pioneer in the psychology of religion in the United States, introducing a course in the subject after teaching ethics and psychology for several years.

One thing reported in common about these philosophers is that they were respected and liked almost unanimously in the university and in Chicago. Their characters and personalities contributed to the spread of the influence of their ideas all over the university and the community and, through their students, all over the country.

T. V. Smith and Edwin A. Burtt were added to the department in 1923, Arthur Murphy in 1927, and Everett Hall in 1929, breaking up the monolithic pragmatism. Moore retired in 1929 and died in 1930 while on a visit to England. Tufts retired as chairman in 1930 but continued to teach half time. Mead was eligible to retire in 1931, but he planned to continue teaching full time in 1931–32. Events, however, took a dramatic turn. While Tufts was still chairman, President Robert M. Hutchins had asked that Mortimer Adler be added to the staff, and Tufts had accepted him. Adler was appointed to a position one-third in philosophy, one-third in psychology, and one-third in law. Then after Mead took over upon Tufts's retirement, Hutchins requested that Scott Buchanan be invited to accept a position in the department for which Hutchins had obtained the promise of funds from outside the university. Mead replied that the department was opposed to complying with the request; and, after consultations within and without the university, including a questionnaire sent to several prominent philosophers, Hutchins agreed to abide by the wishes of the department. Nonetheless, Mead suggested that those who did not concur in Hutchins' views on the department should start looking elsewhere.

Mead himself accepted an appointment at Columbia for 1931–32, but died before he could fill it. Tufts went to the University of California at Los Angeles where he was a lecturer in philosophy until 1933. Burtt, Murphy, and Hall all resigned along with Mead and Tufts, Burtt going to Cornell, Murphy to Brown, and Hall to Ohio State.* Ames remained as pastor of his church and was chairman of the Philosophy Department until 1935. T. V. Smith did not join the exodus, since he had no close ties with the older members of the staff. In fact, by his own account he had been retained on the faculty at the request of members of the university administration rather than of the department.

So the Chicago School came to a definite end in 1931. It seems typical of the University of Chicago that the close of that important era did not take place with the quiet retirement of the remaining patriarchs of the department, after appropriate academic celebrations, but instead was marked by a flurry of resignations amidst considerable uproar, both in the university and in the city. A good pragmatist is never merely a theoretician of action.

The Chicago philosophers vary in the continuing import of their intellectual accomplishments, but they all played roles in their own ways in making the department a School and in making that School one of the most significant and influential in the history of American ideas. The impact of their ideas is still evident in philosophy, education, religion, sociology, and economics, among other fields. The School went when its founders went, but its spirit made a permanent impression on the American intellectual scene, and, in particular, on the vital young university of which it was a central part.

And, while it has been implied that the confluence of men and ideas at Chicago was in a sense a matter of chance, once the cir-

* The account of the last days of the Chicago School was given to me by Professor Arthur Murphy in 1961 at the University of Texas. It has been checked against the records in a volume called *The Faculty of the Division of the Humanities: December 1930–October 1940*; the book is kept in the Secretary of the Faculties Office at the University of Chicago. The entries filed under December 3, 1931, include a "Statement of Professors Mead, Burtt and Murphy" and a report by Gordon J. Laing, dean of the Humanities Division, called "The Situation in the Department of Philosophy."

cumstances converged the success of the venture was no accident. In a famous convocation address, Paul Shorey spoke to this point:

We have been styled a college made to order, or, more graciously, a university by enchantment. And one who merely contemplates the stately panorama of buildings that now occupy what an Aeschylean command of cumulative epithet might describe as the desolate, God-forsaken, weed-grown, mud-splashed, malaria-wrapped, frog-croaking, gander-haunted, cow-pasturing swamp of 1891, may well attribute the transformation to witchcraft and Aladdin's lamp. But we to whom these buildings are but the symbol and the shell of the life they contain, we who know or can divine what it has cost to do the work of a century in seventeen years, we who have shared the travail of creation, borne the shocks of collision and the strain of adjustment in the effort to find ourselves, and awaken at last to the perception that we are not a mere fortuitous concurrence of infinitely repellent particles but a living organism and a collective soul, we can acquiesce in no soulless name for the process that has brought this thing to pass. We ask for words charged wtih humane and moral meanings – generosity, faith, self-sacrifice, courage, devotion, and work.[34]

II

PHILOSOPHY · *A New Foundation*

THE Chicago group represented an important shift in thinking away from belief in a world as a given external reality and mind as a different, internal reality. What had long been viewed as disparate ultimate entities, mind and world, became two factors in a process, necessarily related through the process, neither having any existence independent of the other. Not only does the environment determine the organism, but the organism, in turn, introduces new objects into the environment. In Mead's example, the appearance of an organism capable of digesting grass brings into existence grass as food.

Reaction against the mind-matter dualism was a dominant theme in the development of the functional approach to man's relations to the universe. The British and American idealists had flirted with pragmatic concepts, and James had done much to introduce a theory of process. But the idealists held on to a fixed absolute necessarily distinct from the concrete, partial activities of life, and James clung to something analogous to the soul and its demands upon the world apart from the interactions between the self and the world. The ancient problem of mind and matter had to be solved by dissolving it – dissolving the two forms of being in a stream of activity.

Mind, thought, and consciousness are explained as products of active processes involving a number of agents. There is no isolated individual who must be somehow externally connected with other individuals to form a society. The very process which gives rise to human beings is a social one; hence agents are essentially social beings. The concept of the individual as socially constituted is another side of the concept of mind as receiving its content from the very activity in which it arises, rather than from some external source as in empiricism or from some super-mind as in rationalism.

The world men strive to know and to bring under their control is no longer an array of determinate objects outside the minds of men, toward whose eternal order men's ideas move by accident or magic. The world, as known, is a product of the knowing activity. That activity moves forward to meet new problems raised by new data, and the world as known changes. Each successive theory of the world (including man as part of the world) is accepted because it is more adequate in the face of our problems than previous theories. This does not mean that mind makes the world, any more than that the world makes mind. Thought and objects are equally real, and both are results of the problem-solving activities of organisms. And any set of ideas, together with the world it presents, will yield to other ideas and other worlds in the face of new data and the new problems they bring. Continuity and unity lie in the process by which we come to know the world, not in the nature of the objects known or in the nature of the knowing mind.

The Chicago philosophy derived largely from developments in psychology, just at the time that psychology was beginning in earnest to separate itself in the academic world from philosophy. If psychology was initially subordinated to philosophy departmentally at Chicago, the tail may be said to have wagged the dog in many instances.

Angell, the official department psychologist, stated the dependence of philosophy upon psychology most strongly:

A thorough-going and courageous functional psychology must ultimately issue in investigations which are nowadays the exclusive possessions of logic, ethics, and aesthetics respectively. . . . Either we must suppress functional psychology, or else admit that the so-called ethical examination of the element of value in conduct . . . belongs in reality to the field of functional psychology . . . In

> logic, ethics, and aesthetics we have, therefore, simply systematic developments of problems primarily belonging to a functional psychology. Or, put conversely, functional psychology, if not estopped, must issue in a logic, an ethics, and an aesthetics. . . . If a center of gravity for the detached portions of philosophy be necessary, psychology possesses as a claimant for this honor the notable advantage over its rivals that it is explicitly devoted to the study of the individual as such, from whom all philosophical problems emanate and to whom all solutions of them revert. When this psychological study is interpreted in a functional, as well as in a structural, sense, the theoretical distinctions between psychology and philosophy have ceased to exist.[1]

It is important to note that while psychology seems to have swallowed philosophy in this view, philosophy is still given a necessary existence and relation to psychology. Slightly later, Angell referred to psychology as "the indispensable introduction" to philosophical disciplines.[2] And he again questioned the ground for any distinction between psychology and philosophy other than a practical one of division of labor.

Moore, somewhat less sweeping than Angell, attributed the confusions of modern logic to "the failure thus far to work out the implications of the thoroughly teleological and functional idea which it has accepted from modern psychology." [3] And Dewey talked of psychology as a natural history of psychical events which logic proceeds to judge in terms of their results.[4] Both Dewey and Moore thus presuppose a psychology of a particular sort in their logic, and both refer with approval to Angell's article quoted above.[5] At the beginning, certainly, the psychological laboratories were considered a central part of the Philosophy Department.[6] This, of course, was not due only – or even mainly – to Angell. Dewey's first book was his *Psychology*,[7] and many of Dewey's and Mead's early writings were in psychology. In two early articles,[8] Dewey said that psychology *is* the philosophic method, since consciousness is the whole of reality and psychology is the science of consciousness. These articles are in Dewey's "idealistic period," and by 1903 he would not hold that consciousness is the whole of reality, but I take Moore's reference to the latter of the two as evidence that

Dewey had at least not repudiated the relation stated between psychology and philosophy.[9]

But the most helpful statement of the relation of psychology to philosophy, as the Chicago philosophy developed, is one Mead made in an article entitled "Suggestions toward a Theory of the Philosophical Disciplines." [10] However important certain new psychological concepts may have been for redirecting philosophic inquiries and however essential these men considered turning from metaphysics and epistemology to psychology, psychology never really encompassed the philosophical disciplines for them to the extent that Angell indicated above. Mead's statement is sufficiently important to an understanding of the philosophy of the Chicago School to warrant discussion of it in some detail.

Mead based his article on a concept of sensation he drew from Dewey's article "The Reflex Arc Concept in Psychology": [11] a thing may become a sensation when it becomes problematic, that is, when it has lost objective value and no longer serves as a stimulus to action. Further, it ceases to be a sensation as soon as knowledge of its nature is gained or it ceases to be problematic. The concept of the problematic, as we shall see, becomes the distinguishing mark of the psychical. Mead makes two assumptions and then proceeds to derive the philosophic disciplines from the reflective act. The assumptions are (1) that all analytical thought arises out of a problem and (2) that all reflective thought arises out of real problems and seeks a solution in the form of some means of continuing the activity interrupted by the difficulty.

Dewey's book *How We Think* [12] is an analysis of the act of reflection from a logical point of view. Mead's article is an analysis of that act from the point of view of the rise of the whole range of philosophic problems. He finds that each of the successive stages of the act of reflection yields its peculiar problem. The first stage, that in which the problem in hand is recognized as persistent and demanding solution, is the metaphysical stage. This is the start of the act of reflection, the point at which the problematic element of some ongoing activity demands some kind of alteration in the situation and the nature of the alteration required is uncertain. Mead calls it the metaphysical stage because the question of the reality of the conflicting objects arises here. When action breaks down, the environment of activity loses its objectivity. So long as activity goes along smoothly, there is no question about the reality of objects involved, but objects come into question when the usual reactions to them fail to produce the results desired. The example Dewey uses in "The Reflex Arc Concept in Psychology" illustrates what Mead is talking about: the child who reaches for the candle flame, which to him is simply an attractive bright object, must reconstruct his concept of the object after he gets his fingers burned. The question, as Dewey puts it, is "What kind of bright object is this?" The next bright object the child sees is a questionable object: is this a pretty toy or a hurtful flame? The metaphysical solution to such a problem, Mead says, consists in the assertion of the reality of one idea or system of ideas and the unreality of whatever conflicts with it. In the case of the child, a succession of painful experiences with candle flames would in a normal situation shortly disabuse him of the notion that all bright objects are pleasant toys. He might, however, react to one burn with the idea that all bright objects are hot without being disabused of this notion for some time. By "the real," Mead here intends that which is opposed to the illusory. And the real is determined by whether a consistent pattern of action is possible with regard to the object in question. "Metaphysical reality" in this context is an arbitrary attribution of reality.

Deductive logic appears here as the tool of metaphysics, enabling an organization of the world on the basis of a metaphysical idea or system of ideas to be used to separate the real from the unreal in a methodical manner. If this solution is accepted as final, the act of reflection with respect to reality halts. By means of a deductive system, a theoretical account of the nature of the world can be elaborated with little or no further reference to the practical activities out of which the problem of reality originally arose. On the other hand, if the reality of all the elements of the original conflict is recognized, the act moves to the psychological stage, according to Mead's analysis. And deductive logic may become a general tool for separating for the time being the known elements from the elements to be ignored for the sake of solution of the problem.

In a genuine conflict, all the objects involved can no longer remain objective. Either this difficulty is overcome by a metaphysical solution, in which an arbitrary decision about the nature of the real is imposed upon the problem, or the conflicting elements become subjective. Mead calls this latter alternative the psychological stage of the reflective act. All the elements involved in a problem can play into each other without resistance, in a way they could not so long as they were confined by definite theories and were viewed as objective and conflicting. Control of this play of concepts lies in the necessity of bringing them all together, which means that a new universal encompassing them all must be found to replace the conflicting universals. The process of finding new universals is that of formation of hypotheses and verification of them, which process we call inductive logic. In the psychological stage, the elements in the conflict have no objective validity. They are purely psychical and, in Mead's words, "absolutely *sui generis* in the life of the individual." They regain objectivity only when a solution is hit upon and proved to the extent that the activity halted can continue.

If we expand the process described above from the particular problem at hand to conduct as a whole, we move to the ethical stage of the reflective act. Freedom, from Mead's standpoint, can be defined in terms of the identification of the whole self with the problem and its solution. Obligation lies in the necessity to act and the claim of the whole self for representation in the act. An ethical solution becomes one in which all tendencies are taken into account so far as is possible. Identification of the self with one set of tendencies as against others gives rise to conflict which is chronic, not just a step in a process of natural development. Ethics then is concerned with the constant search for more inclusive universals as solutions for the conflicts that arise in experience, this expanding universality giving ever fuller possibilities for expression of all the positive tendencies of the self.

Short of a new universal, a psychical solution to a problem may yield new meanings of sensuous objects. These objects then take on representative or aesthetic value. The artist gives the conditions for solution of his problem in some sensuous form. His statement lends to effort the enjoyment of an end not yet attained (perhaps even unattainable under present conditions). He objectifies in artistic form values that cannot yet be made real in the ordinary commerce of life. The step beyond giving these unattained objects artistic (therefore artificial) reality carries us into religion, wherein reality of a more comprehensive sort is attributed to these objects as bearers of the meaning and value of life.

General theory of logic, finally, deals with the whole process of reflective thought and with the place of each of the stages discussed above within the process. In terms of thought it is concerned with the passage of the whole objective world from an unanalyzed state through the reflective act back into unanalyzed reality again.

Thus in Mead's treatment, although starting from a psychological idea, we are led to an analysis that results in psychology being dealt with as the result of one stage in the total process of the act of reflection. The various philosophical disciplines are shown as integrally related but sufficiently distinguished to warrant their existence as distinct disciplines. It is easy to see how the psychologist who discovers the functional nature of the act in the psychical stage of the act and sees the implications of this discovery for both earlier and later stages could attribute an architectonic role to psychology. Only as he moved from any individual stage to the general theory of logic would psychology fall into the perspective indicated in Mead's analysis. And the Chicago philosophers did just that: they moved from a central concern with psychology to concern with logical theory. At the same time, they could retain an interest in psychology as *part* of the total concept of the act. The psychologists, on the other hand, continuing their interest in the psychical stage alone, gradually ceased mentioning the relation of psychology to philosophy and looked from psychology in the direction of physiology and anatomy as a means of carving out their particular bailiwick.

This break (or separation) of psychology from philosophy proceeded fairly rapidly. A separate Psychology Department was formed in 1905 with Angell as its head. In his 1912 book,[13] Angell makes one brief mention of philosophy, as he does in his 1918 volume.[14]

But we are here concerned with the broad philosophic views represented at Chicago, and we will proceed to examine them in the order set forth in the Mead treatment above. This is not to imply that all the Chicago scholars or even philosophers necessarily agreed with Mead's analysis, but his framework does give a scheme for dealing with the various aspects of the Chicago position, and differences of opinion can be brought out as we proceed within that framework.

1. The revolt against dualism was a revolt against a bad metaphysics — hence against a philosophic framework that gave rise to false problems and misleading solutions. According to the functionalist account of experience, mind and matter, subject and object, person and world are methodological abstractions. So long as they are used with reference to the context out of which they arose, they are both useful and meaningful. But the epistemologists, both empirical and rational, have wrenched these abstractions out of their particular problematic context and erected them into ontological concepts. Such abstractions cut off from the dynamic, historic situation that gave them birth are without any meaningful reference, and the result is the artificial problem of knowledge that has plagued philosophy since Descartes. More generally, Dewey referred to the false sense of metaphysics as a general idea which remains remote from contact with actual experience.[15] Such a general idea cannot identify the real precisely because it remains abstract and resists all effort at concrete embodiment.

It might seem to follow that if mind and matter are not designations of the real in any absolute sense, perhaps experience is. Moore does, in fact, state that experience conceived as "a process the results of which at any given point constitute the material for and stimulus to further activity" is accepted as "our 'ultimate reality.' "[16] Elsewhere he says that reality lies in experience.[17] And the latter view seems to be the one usually cited by the Chicago group. In "Psychology as Philosophic Method" (1886), Dewey says that consciousness is the sole content, account and criterion of all reality." The term "consciousness" later is replaced by "experience" as the term inclusive of reality.[18] This coincides with Mead's analysis in that reality is considered within the reflective act, hence within experience. But this further means that reality is not a fixed category but shifts with shifting contexts, and traditional metaphysical distinctions are erected only by discarding the context. In keeping with the historic, dynamic treatment of experience, reality is pluralistic rather than dualistic or monistic. Dewey distinguishes this pluralism from James's "bare pluralism" or "disconnection." [19] The various reals are related to each other within the act of reflection. What this amounts to, as Dewey later put it, is that "things . . . are what they are experienced as." [20] A sudden noise in the night, to use his example, really is fearsome. If a subsequent experience proves that the noise is that of a flapping window shade and hence not fearsome, then the later experience may be truer than the first one, but it is not more real. Dewey is concerned in this discussion to set forth the complexity of experience. Any object is different as given in a knowing experience, an aesthetic experience, a moral experience, etc. These different perspectives can be related to each other only as the different kinds of experience involved can be related.

Mead states the position in terms closer to the traditional distinction between the constant and the transitory. Enduring things are those which remain unchanged in our conduct for some time within the perspective of our group. Mead points out that a metaphysics that extracts these elements and gives them subsistential being forgets that the endurance in question is strictly relative to the particular social situation. The real as against the illusory is a methodological distinction, just as mind and matter or subject and object is.[21]

This still seems to leave unanswered the question whether or not experience or some corresponding concept is the Real. Mead's general theory of logic might appear to be his term for metaphysics, since he says that the general theory deals with the whole objective world in thought terms and since the other philosophic disciplines are derived from the logical analysis of the reflective act. But he explicitly sidesteps any such interpretation in a revealing passage following another mention of the analysis of the functions of the act:

It is, of course, possible to make this a metaphysical doctrine. If one finds reality in immediate experience and admits that the various intellectual, aesthetic, and perceptual processes exist only as parts and functions of an act which is the ultimate form of immediate experience, then the recognition of the ethical statement of this act as its fullest statement would found metaphysics upon ethics. The presentation of such a doctrine, however, would demand first of all a discussion of the meaning of the terms "immediate experience," of "reality," and the "cognitive state" that answers to it. I have no wish to enter this debatable field, that is loosely defined by the term pragmatism.[22]

The act cannot be termed the ultimate form of experience because over against the problematic area within which reflection takes place stands the whole unquestioned, unanalyzed world that is simply there and to which we must bring any hypothesis or new universal for its test. This world that is simply there cannot be said to be known, but it also cannot be said to be unreal since all knowledge must be referred to that world for validation. Therefore the act situation does not constitute the whole of reality.[23] Is the world that is there, then, the world of experience in its widest sense, and is this world the Real? Certainly the world is *there* only as it is experienced in some sense, but, again, the real (as opposed to the Real) is found *in* experience and more particularly in the reflective act, for the reason that questions of reality arise only within that context. The question of the Real does not arise, because there is no reflective act in general: all reflection is concrete and particular. The analysis of the act can be generalized, but particular categories arising from analysis of the act of reflection hold only for that particular kind of act and situation and cannot be extended beyond. In the beginning at least, the Chicagoans preferred not to plunge into metaphysical questions any further than was necessary to discredit past metaphysical dogmas. Dewey speaks for the whole movement when he says: "Philosophy, defined as such a logic [of experience], makes no pretense to be an account of a closed and finished universe. Its business is not to secure or guarantee any particular reality or value. *Per contra*, it gets the significance of a method." [24] The real, just as the true and the valuable, is to be disclosed by inquiry; disclosed for the particular problematic situation and its solution. And the solution ends the problematic situation and dissolves the metaphysical questions raised. This is a thoroughgoing relativism. The totality of experience cannot be spoken of as real, since there is nothing to set over against it as unreal. The implications of this opposition to all absolutes for a variety of fields will be seen farther on.

2. Philosophical psychology, according to Mead, has to do with the internalized aspects of the reflective act. Or in Angell's words, "mental facts, or facts of consciousness, constitute the field of psychology." [25] An element becomes mental or psychical only when it ceases to function objectively, that is, as an immediate stimulus. Mind, or the psyche, is a *behavioristic* concept, identified by distinct modes of acting. James had still talked of mind as an object in his *Psychology* and was concerned with relating the mind as object to other objects.[26] The functionalists abandoned the psyche as an object and concerned themselves with the psychical act. "The sensation or conscious stimulus is not a thing or existence by itself; it is that phase of a coordination requiring attention because, by reason of the conflict within the coordination, it is uncertain how to complete it. . . . Just here the act as objective stimulus becomes transformed into sensation as possible, as conscious, stimulus." [27] Similarly, the idea appears when the "perfect continuity of stimulation, present in the habit form of activity," is interrupted by some discontinuity in the activity.[28] The idea exists as a plan of action for the construction of a new object or a new universal that will permit the resumption of the activity. Emotion, too, appears as a consequence of inner struggle and inhibition.[29] Experience becomes internal or subjective only when it becomes problematic; otherwise the interactions of the organism and the environment occur without involving anything that could be called mental. And in the problematic situation, the mental is not a different kind of

existence: it is a psychological distinction made within experience as a way of dealing with one stage of problem-solving activity. Myron Ashley put it this way: "Sensory quality marks the point of stress, or seeming arrest, while the ideal or imaged aspect defines the continuing activity as projected, and hence that with which start is to be made in coping with the obstacle. . . . The sensation stands for the interrupted habit, while the image stands for the new habit, that is, the new way of dealing with the subject-matter." [30]

Functional psychology called itself behavioristic, but it shortly had to distinguish itself from the behaviorism of John B. Watson, who was one of the early products of the Chicago Psychology Department. Automatic or habitual behavior would fall under psychology in the later behaviorism, but only behavior involving psychical elements would fall under functionalism.

The functional psychologist proper would be concerned with the experimental determination of the facts of vision, audition, learning, and such. The philosopher corresponding to this functional position is interested in such facts as the psychologist discovers for their bearing on an understanding of the psychical phase of the reflective act. This phase is of vital importance in explaining the progression from the emergence of a problem in an act situation to a successful solution of that problem.

By and large, the Chicago philosophers, after the first few years of joint endeavor with the psychologists, were interested in psychology mainly as a statement of the nature of the psychical stage of the act. Mead is an exception; he continued an interest in psychology as such and devoted much of his energies to the development of a social psychology. *Mind, Self and Society* is the fullest statement we have of the results of that effort. Mead's psychology remains philosophical in that it is worked out in terms of the categories derived from the act. It is not experimental as much as conceptual, although Mead tried to take into account the results of contemporary experiments in psychology. Mead presents in detailed analysis the development out of a prior, unconscious social situation of gestures, language, self-consciousness, mind, self, and human society. By internalizing the language of gestures, by developing the ability to call out in himself the same response his gestures call out in others, man has become capable of using anticipated results of action to guide present action. This capability constitutes the peculiarly human intelligence or power of reflection. By taking the attitudes of others toward his own conduct, the individual becomes an object to himself, and it is as he is able to take an objective, nonemotional view of himself that the individual becomes self-conscious and capable of reason. For Mead, then, the reflective act comes into being within a broad social process which can itself be accounted for only by a theory of biological evolution. Social psychology is the framework within which a general theory of logic would take shape as the theory of reflection.

Dewey, too, continues an interest in psychology, but his *How We Think* was a logic of the processes of reflection and his *Human Nature and Conduct* was in his own words an introduction to a social psychology and not itself such a psychology. Dewey's later interest in psychology was in its bearing on logical and moral problems. When the psychology laboratory was removed from the Philosophy Department the break was more than a physical one. The fact remains, however, that the later developments stemmed from the initial atmosphere of cooperation and common effort and continued to show results of that early conjunction of interests.

3. Ethics undertakes to evaluate the reflective act with relation to the whole context of the act situation. Dewey defines ethics as "the science of conduct, understanding by conduct man's activity in its whole reach." [31] He goes on to say that the business of ethics is "to detect the element of obligation in conduct, to see what gives it its *worth*." And, typically, the main point of agreement among the Chicago philosophers is that any ethical standard or principle or imperative must come from within the act situation itself. In fact, Dewey's first philosophic use of the term "function" occurs in his *Outlines of a Critical Theory of Ethics* as the category uniting the agent and the environment or the internal and the external aspects of conduct. The basis for evaluation of action lies in the interaction between organism and environment. The statement of this basis varied from fairly orthodox moral terminology to strictly bi-

ological terminology, but the conception of something corresponding to function or interaction remained central.[32]

The ethical problem presents itself in one of two ways: as the problem of evaluating ends within the process of the act or as the problem of evaluating the entire process. These reduce to the same problem, however, since ends within the act can be judged only in reference to action as a whole. The moral problem is a conflict of ends, interests, values. Stuart puts it in traditional terms: "there are cases in which the emergence of the end forthwith is followed by a check to the reflective process, and the agent shrinks from the end presented in imagination as being, let us say, one forbidden by authority or one repugnant to his own established standards." [33] The conflict of ends may take the more prosaic form of a clash of ends both of which are recognized as values but which circumstances make incompatible. The problem is to find a resolution of the conflict, whatever form the conflict may take.

Charles Morris, in his introduction to *Mind, Self and Society*, says that all pragmatists since James have held an interest theory of value: "that is good which satisfies an interest or impulse." [34] However, this concept of interest requires some qualification in order to make sense of the moral theories of Mead and Dewey. James talks about interests as demands or claims which exist just because some sentient being happens to feel them; and he talks of the settlement of conflicts of claims in terms of greater and smaller demands. He holds that social demand is stronger than individual demands because it is more inclusive of the total set of demands. The demands of God would be the strongest of all. Yet James's disclaimer of any pragmatic criterion in morals ("The nobler thing *tastes* better, and that is all that we can say"),[35] leaves us with no clear basis for judging the relative merits (or strengths) of the particular demands that pose our moral problems. The Chicago brand of pragmatism took a more consistent view. Mead, for instance, does speak of a moral solution to a problem as one that recognizes all values and impulses.[36] In a later record, he calls a categorical imperative the demand that one should act with reference to all the interests involved in a moral situation.[37] But since interests make up the content of moral judgments, something other than interests alone must serve as a criterion for judgment and action in the face of conflicting interests or interests that are unfulfillable. Interests are rejected as well as accepted in the process of evaluation, as Mead makes clear in his discussion of the need for the individual to expand his social awareness: "One is constituted out of his own interests; and when those interests are frustrated, what is called for then is in some sense a sacrifice of this narrow self. This should lead to the development of a larger self which can be identified with the interests of others . . . the person who does that does not really sacrifice himself, but becomes a larger self." [38] All the interests involved in a moral problem enter into an adequate solution:

Doing this thing, buying this particular object, means that you shall not do this, that, or the other thing. State the thing you are going to do in terms of the things you cannot do, so that they are clearly presented in their relation to one another — that is the fundamental thing in the ethical situation. Be able to state that this particular good thing means not doing something else, so that you evaluate them in terms of each other. . . . Now, you should not in any ethical problem leave out of account any end; even if it means a sacrifice, your conduct has to acknowledge that and take it into account. You give up something of value, and your conduct ought to recognize that value. Your final hypothesis, then, must take into account all the values involved.[39]

The criterion for evaluating an act or a person or an end is the act situation itself. An interest has an object; it is *in* an object. And objects are judged as good or bad as they tend to expand and enrich interests and action or the reverse. Dewey states it in this way: "As natural science found its outlet by admitting no idea, no theory, as fixed by itself, demanding of every idea that it become fruitful in experiment, so must ethical science purge itself of all conceptions, of all ideals, save those which are developed within and for the sake of practice." [40] The more interests satisfied, the more objects realized. And the more objects realized, the broader base the agent has for further action in new situations.

Man must act, and therein lies the basis of moral obligation. For only in recognizing the claims of the whole self, the demands of all the interests involved, can action be expansive rather than constricting. Selfishness means acting for a past or fixed self, acting for those things that have been proved beneficial to the self, instead of acting in terms of present requirements of action.[41] Action that takes into account the total situation that calls for action by trying to harmonize all the claims insofar as they can be harmonized is moral action. Seizing upon one set of interests or impulses in the self as being representative of the "true" self as opposed to other interests leads, in Mead's words, to chronic internal moral conflict. Overlooking the social nature of the self will lead to external conflict. And the essential social nature of the moral situation is the heart of the moral views of the Chicago School.

Man is not merely gregarious by instinct nor does he form societies to satisfy any such instinct. Man is a self-conscious, reflective being because he develops the power of reflection and his self-awareness out of a social situation, a situation of interaction with other beings of the same kind, out of an ongoing system of gestures and responses that exists before his awareness of them or himself. Therefore man is not atomic; neither are his interests or his impulses. He and all that makes him up are thoroughly social. Action always involves other persons, and to ignore the other persons involved in an act is to ignore the most fundamental parts of the act situation. "That there is such a thing as a conduct at all means that there are certain beings who have acquired definite ways of responding to one another. It is important to observe that these forms of interaction — instinct and habit, perception, memory, etc. — are not to be located in either of the interacting beings but are functions of both."[42] Moore spells out what this functional interpretation means when he says that pragmatism "presupposes that 'my' thinking and feeling may be as truly a function of 'your' brain or mind as of my own. My thinking of sending for you as a physician to treat my headache is as truly a function of your medically trained brain as of my own aching one. And 'your' thinking as you diagnose my case is no less obviously a function of my head than of your own."[43]

A moral ideal, then, grows out of the moral situation, the problem and its particular circumstances. It cannot, as moral, be imposed from outside the situation by man or God. Since the moral situation is always social, the ideal must be social. The ideal is a statement not only of what is required to restore harmony in the immediate circumstances but also of the relation of this action to the larger world of action in which this act takes place. The ideal in a given situation may be unattainable under the circumstances and yet remain as an end to be striven for as changing circumstances permit. Some ideals may be erected into permanent objectives, objectives considered sufficiently valuable to hold on to in spite of the fact that their full attainment has to be continually postponed in the hope of more propitious circumstances. Acting upon such an ideal would largely be acting to bring about those more promising circumstances. These postponed ideals may be political, religious, or aesthetic. Democracy is such an objective, preserved in the form of our political institutions even though it is almost never achieved. The religious goal of the brotherhood of man is another, maintained more or less in our churches full in the face of man's inhumanity to man. A world of beauty encompassing all activities of man is cherished (at least sporadically) as a vision by art and letters. All of these ideals, however, imply an Ideal determined by the very nature of the practical. This Ideal obviously cannot be the frozen absolute of complete accomplishment of all ends: there would be no room for practice or thought or appreciation inside such a totality. The ideal of *practice* must be one of the intelligence to deal with constantly changing problems, of means for control of varying conditions, and of character to adapt to and grow with the possibilities being developed in the world. All other ideals derive from this one for this brand of pragmatism. It is true that Dewey, Mead, Moore, and others shy away from much explicit discussion of this overarching ideal. Their emphasis is always on the specific, the particular, the concrete. And they fear the constant threat that an end held under a peculiar set of historical circumstances will be erected into The End for man and become with the passing of the circumstances a millstone around men's necks, dragging them away from the demands of new problems. Note

Dewey's early statement of this concern: "It is of the very nature of moral conduct to be progressive. Permanence of *specific* ideals means moral death. . . . The realization of moral ends must bring about a changed situation, so that the repetition of the same ends would no longer satisfy."[44] But this Ideal is just beneath the surface in almost all their ethical writings. It is most obvious in the various analyses of the act. Mead works this Ideal out in most detail in *Mind, Self and Society* and *The Philosophy of the Act*, yet the closest he comes to explicit statement of it is in the following passages:

> We are all of us in some sense changing the social order in which we belong; our very living does it, and we ourselves change as we go on; there is always action to answer to reaction in the social world. That process of continuing reconstruction is the process of value, and the only essential imperative I can see is that this essential social process has got to go on — the community, on the one hand, and the selves that make up the community. It has to continue not so much because the happiness of all is worth more than the happiness of the individual but, being what we are, we have to continue being social beings, and society is essential to the individual just as the individual is essential to society. That relationship has to be kept up, and the problem is how the essential social values involved can be maintained.[45]

> So, looking at happiness from the point of view of impulses themselves, we can set up a standard in this fashion: the end should be one which reinforces the motive, one which will reinforce the impulse and expand other impulses or motives. That would be the standard proposed.[46]

The first passage indicates that our ends must accord with the conditions of the social process, whether we state those conditions in terms of the community or of the individuals who make up the community. The second interprets those conditions from the individual's standpoint. In the latter vein, Stuart talks of the concept of the self as, not an ideal content, but a general principle of moral experimentation.[47] In the former vein, Dewey says that the standard of action is not absolute in rigid statement but is absolute in never-failing application to the changing problems of the moral world.[48]

There is no set of fixed values because values are determined by conduct and conduct alters constantly. The values being realized by this act will alter the possibilities of value achievement for future conduct. Hence, from this point of view, we cannot discuss the value of action as such. Man *is* an acting being. Ethics cannot judge this fact as good or bad. Men have no basis for an over-all judgment that the game, in the abstract, is worth the candle; the whole point of instrumental ethics is that the values realized in action can *make* the game worth the candle. Even those ideals most remote from realization, if they function as true ideals, arise out of activity and serve to make activity richer here and now. Just as men cannot hold experience to be real as against something not experience and not real, but can only distinguish reals within experience, so they cannot appraise action itself as good or bad but can only judge kinds of action and ends in the light of their essential action involvement.

Perhaps it should be stressed that this outlook does not imply that life and action are necessarily uninterrupted series of triumphs by man. The pragmatists in general have been condemned as wild optimists, and they are in general optimistic about the possibilities for man. They insist that increasing awareness of his role in shaping his world will increase man's chances for shaping it to his heart's desire. But these men weren't blind to the nature of life and the world; they knew the difference between possibilities and actualities. Such values as we do attain, we attain through action. Many values we fail to attain fully or in part, sometimes because of errors in acting, sometimes because of conditions that are outside our control.[49]

The ideal that the Chicagoans do mention frequently is that of democracy. One of the vital results for them of the abandonment of all forms of absolutism and status was the democratization of philosophy in general. The individual has the right to judge his own experience – and the responsibility to seek adequate standards for judgment. But adequate standards cannot be external; they cannot come from the heritage of the past, although a heritage is indispensable for the formation of standards; neither can they come from the wise or the expert or those in authority. Standards must come from the course of experience that gives rise to the demand for them. And this is the "heart of the ethical significance of the whole anti-absolute movement. It is the democratic movement in morals; it is the demand for the *full* conditions of moral responsibility. It is the claiming of the moral franchise, — the right to participate in the construction as well as the execution of the ideal." [50] Dewey stated the democratic ideal with reference to personality in an early monograph:

There is an individualism in democracy which there is not in aristocracy; but it is an ethical, not a numerical individualism; it is an individualism of freedom, of responsibility, of initiative to and for the ethical ideal, not an individualism of lawlessness. In one word, democracy means that *personality* is the first and final reality. It admits that the full significance of personality can be learned by the individual only as it is already presented to him in objective form in society; it admits that the chief stimuli and encouragements to the realization of personality come from society; but it holds, none the less, to the fact that personality cannot be procured for any one, however degraded and feeble, by any one else, however wise and strong. It holds that the spirit of personality indwells in every individual and that the choice to develop it must proceed from that individual.[51]

Mead modified this personal ideal and states the way the ideal of democracy functions politically:

Furthermore, there are many values involved in our problems of social conduct to which we feel that we are unable to do justice in their whole import, and yet when they are once envisaged they appear too precious to be ignored, so that in our action we do homage to them. We do not do justice to them. They constitute our ideals. They abide in our conduct as prophecies of the day in which we can do them the justice they claim. They take on the form of institutions that presuppose situations which we admit are not realized, but which *demand* realization.

Such an ideal is democracy written into our governmental institutions. . . . There cannot be self-government until there can be an intelligent will expressed in the community, growing out of the intelligent attitudes of the individuals and groups in whose experience the community exists. Our institutions are in so far democratic that when a public sentiment is definitely formed and expressed it is authoritative. But an authoritative public sentiment upon a public issue is very infrequent. . . .

However, we are unwilling to surrender the ideal of such a government, if only for the sake of the exceptional occasions upon which it is realized, but more profoundly because we cherish the hope that the form of the institution in some way helps toward the realization of what it promises.[52]

Ethics deals with conduct as a whole, whereas psychology deals with one stage of the reflective act and general theory of logic deals with the act in relation to scientific investigation. There is nothing surprising in the fact that ethics should be architectonic for a philosophy of action.

4. Art is the process of representing ideals (which remain ideal in conduct, at least in part) in some objective form, as audible, visible, tangible objects. The aesthetic object thus embodies an idea, but since the idea cannot be fully accomplished in action, the object must also embody feeling, emotion, and sensation to produce a wholeness, a completeness of experience that actual conduct never attains. The Greek statue represents a perfection of the human being that no actual individual can reach. Yet it stands as an embodiment in relatively permanent form of physical and spiritual harmony. It abstracts from the physical and moral flaws of real men – it is an ideal man made visible and tangible. In Dewey's words: "Active art is the embodiment of ideals; the clothing of ideas otherwise abstract in their peculiar and fit garb of concrete outward detail; passive art is the quick and accurate response to such embodiments as are already made." [53] Typically, however, art grows out of conduct, out of the ordinary affairs of life. As Tufts points out, the aesthetic is essentially social, and art objects are produced initially for economic, protective, sexual, military, magical, ceremonial, religious, and intellectual purposes. Art appreciation comes only after such objects have been produced for practical reasons.[54] And aesthetic activity that is divorced from the life around it fails of any truly aesthetic purpose. Ideals that are meaningful grow out of action prompted by concrete problems, and the

true artist embodies the ideals that exist in the struggles going on in the society in which he lives. This does not mean that ideals cannot transcend any particular time and its troubles, but it does mean that ideals that are not mere empty flights of fancy must grow out of some time and its troubles. For Dewey, art emerges even more concretely from problems of craftsmanship in the production of useful articles.

> I think everybody who has not a purely literary view of the subject recognizes that genuine art grows out of the work of the artisan. The art of the Renaissance was great, because it grew out of the manual arts of life. It did not spring up in a separate atmosphere, however ideal, but carried on to their spiritual meaning processes found in homely and everyday forms of life. . . . The merely artisan side is narrow, but the mere art, taken by itself, and grafted on from without, tends to become forced, empty, sentimental. . . . All art involves physical organs, the eye and hand, the ear and voice; and yet it is something more than the mere technical skill required by the organs of expression. It involves an idea, a thought, a spiritual rendering of things; and yet it is other than any number of ideas by themselves. It is a living union of thought and the instrument of expression.[55]

Further, the aesthetic is not limited to the contemplation of a completed art object. The artisan who, in addition simply to getting on with the job, appreciates the balance and form of his tools and their peculiar fitness for the job in hand has an aesthetic sense of his work. And he may have imported into every stage of his activity an awareness and appreciation of the end toward which he is working, so as to give an aesthetic cast to the entire process. All work should, ideally, take such an aesthetic form. But, as Mead points out in a reworking of his views on the aesthetic stage:

> . . . those that can import the aesthetic experience into activity must be fortunately engaged and engaged in rewarding undertakings. And this means more than the mere adaptation of means to end, the mere successful cooperative fashioning of the goods which are enjoyed in common. The enjoyment of its ultimate use must be suggested by the intermediate steps in its production, and flow naturally into the skill which constructs it. It is this which gives joy to creation, and belongs to the work of the artist, the research sci-

entist, and the skilled artisan who can follow his article through to its completion. It belongs to co-ordinated efforts of many, when the role of the other in the production is aroused in each worker at the common task, when the sense of team play, esprit de corps, inspires interrelated activities. In these situations something of the delight of consummation can crown all intermediate processes.

It is unfortunately absent from most labor in a modern competitive industrial society. But the thirst for enjoyment is still there, and the imagination, deprived of its normal function.[56]

Beauty, then, is the ideal of complete, harmonious adaptation in life of means to ends and of ends to each other, as that ideal is given sensuous existence. Aesthetics is the science that deals with the norms or standards of beauty, just as logic deals with the norms of truth and ethics with the norms of good.*

Art gives ideals sensuous form, but in so doing makes them artificial, in a sense removes them from the field of action. The painting requires a frame to distinguish it from its surroundings. The aesthetic can permeate action and enrich it, but the very completeness of the aesthetic experience itself sets it off from action proper. Men may go beyond the artistic representation of ideals to a belief in the reality of them, but this is the realm of religion. Mead says, "The religious consciousness is pre-eminently one that recognizes in life a fundamental problem, while it clings to the reality of the great representative objects of conduct which the conflict has abstracted and set before us." [57] Art must arrest action in order to capture the values inherent in experience; religion frees those values by giving them a reality. Tufts puts it that "it is the task of religion to quicken the appreciation for that which is none the less real because its reality is experienced within consciousness, and not located outside of it." [58]

In general, the members of the Chicago School shied away from

* Henry W. Stuart disagrees with this view of aesthetics. In his "Valuation as a Logical Process" in *Studies in Logical Theory* (Chicago: University of Chicago Press, 1903), he calls the aesthetic experience post-judgmental appreciation. The only values he recognizes are economic (having to do with means) and ethical (having to do with ends). He gives art no real role in constructing reality, as Dewey, Mead, and Tufts do; hence aesthetics is not a value science. See especially pp. 339–40 of his essay.

any real development of the themes of religion, just as they did from formal logics, and for much the same reason. The traditional concepts of religion and the historical cults of religion were too closely associated with ways of thinking and acting from which these men were actively dissociating themselves, as were the concepts and systems of deductive logics of the past. Ames, of course, was an exception. But Ames is not typical of the early developments in the School in this regard, and he will be discussed in detail later in connection with the influence of the movement on religious theories outside the central circle of philosophers we are here concerned with.

One thing is clear: whatever religion may be otherwise, it is derived from ethics and is essentially an extension of ethical ideals. Both Dewey and Mead discuss Christianity as a moral doctrine and give it historical importance as the bearer of certain social principles.[59]

5. The new psychology implied a new philosophy; and a new philosophy required a new organon. Hence an instrumental logic was developed for use in attacking one citadel after another of the old empiricisms and idealisms. Dewey led his colleagues and students in an all-out attack on the logics of idealism and sensationism and in an exploration of the logic of pragmatism.

Not much attention was given to deductive logic in the new approaches. As we saw, Mead attributed the appearance of deductive logic to the metaphysical stage of the act of reflection. Deduction was associated with classification and the erection of hierarchies and was a means of separating the real from the illusory, the true from the false, and the good from the bad — all in relation to fixed, eternal, absolute standards. Angell represents deduction as the application of a mental habit to a particular case, as opposed to induction, which is the process of the formation of these habits.[60] And certainly the emphasis of functionalism is on the formative process rather than on the application of established habit patterns. But since the distinction between using and forming habits in a world in flux is one of degree rather than of kind, deduction and induction are never entirely separated except under some sort of external restraint. Thus Mead recognizes that deduction is used throughout any experimental procedure, but he says that we characterize as entirely deductive those procedures in which we deal with problems whose solutions are rendered taboo by social circumstances. Therefore deduction is associated with the method of dealing with problems marked insoluble because solution threatens the social status.[61] In other words, in the solution of any problem we necessarily rely upon habits and principles based on past experience; but solutions to new problems cannot be arrived at without deserting old forms for new hypotheses. When we are afraid to desert the old ways of thinking, mind and action become stagnant; and this stagnancy, which is associated with clinging to habit and so with deduction, is the reason for stressing formation and testing of hypothesis rather than the past experience upon which such formation rests. Deduction is necessary and useful if we but desert the metaphysical mode of thinking and use deduction as an instrument for solving problems instead of as a means of getting rid of any fact or idea that does not fit our preconceptions of the world. Deductive elaboration of a hypothesis permits careful testing of that hypothesis by focusing attention on what is essential to *this* solution, but it does not utter any finalities about reality or truth or value. Reality or truth or value is established only by processes of experience that go beyond the deductive stage.

Deduction originates as a tool in the metaphysical stage of reflection, and induction originates as a tool in the psychological stage. Induction is the process of formation of new mental habits, to permit interrupted action to continue, formation of new universals to re-establish harmony in our experience, or formation and testing of hypotheses for the solution of problems. One aspect of this process we can say little about, either logically or psychologically: that is the actual procedure by which a new universal or hypothesis is seized upon. This, as Mead says, is the realm of the genius for suggestion. Myron Ashley attempts an explanation of the origin of hypotheses,[62] but he merely restates the *role* of hypotheses in logical and psychological terms. More can be and is said about the process of verifying an idea once it has been hit upon. Here the functionalist makes much of the constant interplay between hypothesis and experiment as they mutually determine each other until they coalesce in a solution that meets all the requirements of the present situation. And not only must each successive experiment or observation render the hypothesis in question more probable, it must at the same time show alternative possibilities less probable or improbable. In an analogous fashion, the finding of similar cases is never sufficient for an induction; unlike cases must also be found. Only similarity in the midst of dissimilarity is in any sense conclusive evidence for an idea.[63]

The main logical interest at Chicago, however, was not in deduction or induction as such but in a logical theory which opposed the concept of a fixed world of reality to which the mind tried to accommodate its thoughts. It was in logical theory that the metaphysical problem mentioned above was really met head on. And it is in the field of logical theory that Dewey made his most distinctive contribution to the Chicago School. Dewey's lectures and seminars on logic marked the turning from a primary concern with psychology to the broader fields of philosophy. This can be seen, for instance, in the movement through logic into ethics, economics, and metaphysics in the *Studies in Logical Theory*. Moore remarks upon the importance of this change in *Pragmatism and Its Critics*:

> So long as pragmatism was in its "psychological" stage and contented itself with observing that all ideas are purposive, we merely exclaimed, "How interesting!" But when some adventurous souls began to carry the implications of this psychology over into logic and ethics, into metaphysics and theology, and to point out the discrepancies between it and the current conception of truth and error, of right and wrong, and of God, the plot began to thicken; alarums were sounded; signals were hoisted; cobwebbed armor and weapons were seized, and the most active campaign in philosophy since Kant was on.[64]

Dewey early set the conditions in logical terms for the solution of the metaphysical problem of kinds of reality: "To me it seems as if the judgment of the mind were, for logic, the primary fact, and as if the distinction between the idea and the fact were one which takes place within and on account of the judgment — the logical process."[65] In *Studies in Logical Theory*, he explores this logical process as arising out of concrete problems within an on-going pre-logical activity. Thought appears only with some sort of interference in activity. But Dewey does not restrict logic to thought alone. He discriminates "logic in its wider sense, concerned with the sequence of characteristic functions and attitudes in experience, from logic in its stricter meaning, concerned in particular with description and interpretation of the function of reflective thought."[66] He goes on to say that we cannot isolate one of these senses of logic from the other. Logic cannot account for reflection apart from the position of reflection in experience.

In *How We Think* Dewey summarizes the stages in an act of thought: "(i) a felt difficulty; (ii) its location and definition; (iii) suggestions of possible solution; (iv) development by reasoning of the bearings of the suggestion; (v) further observation and experiment leading to its acceptance or rejection; that is, the conclusion of belief or disbelief."[67] Stage (ii) is Mead's metaphysical stage; (iii) and (iv) correspond to his psychological stage, while (iii) involves mainly induction and (iv) deduction; (v) is the action required for verification and leading, depending upon the circumstances, to ethical, aesthetic, or religious ideals.

Whatever logical elements one finds are found within this problem-solving activity. Whatever rules or criteria are devised must be devised as internal to this same activity. The sensations and ideas thought uses come into being in the thought process, and any principles that really are to serve a logical purpose will result from applying the process of inquiry to inquiry itself.*

A relatively unified pre-logical experience is broken up or disorganized so that the flow of the experience halts. Out of this

* Consistently, Dewey says that general theories of logic appear only when traditional notions no longer serve in enabling thought to deal with the problems that arise. The inadequacy of prior logics in accounting for the actual procedures and products of science constituted just such a disruption between thought and what were accepted as the rules of thought. See *Studies in Logical Theory*, pp. 3–9. On the question of the historical development of logic, see Dewey, "Some Stages of Logical Thought," *Philosophical Review*, 9 (no. 5):465–89 (September 1900); reprinted in *Essays in Experimental Logic* (Chicago: University of Chicago Press, 1916; reissued New York: Dover, 1953).

broken-up experience portions are isolated as sense data or the given of the situation and portions as meanings or possible reactions. From this standpoint, meanings are instruments for the reconstruction of the disrupted experience. What is needed is the selection, from the meanings found in the situation, of those that will coalesce with the sense data and permit a new unification of experience. Meaning and existence are distinctions made within a particular situation and are not fixed distinctions. In a different situation, an existence may become a meaning and vice versa. What emerges from this process of the restoration of the wholeness of experience as an idea or a concept is a tendency or habit of thought. An idea is the tendency or tendencies to think of certain subject matters in relation to each other and to other subject matters in certain ways. Mead says that an idea is "a whole series of possible responses." [68] The term "dog," for instance, tends to call out a group of responses. A dog may be a playmate, an enemy, a hunting companion and helper, a guardian, a property object, or any of a number of other things. One's idea of a dog is the sum of the tendencies that particular term calls out.

On this problematic interpretation of thought, truth is measured by the degree to which a selection of meanings does restore the unity of experience. Thought emerges out of a whole of experience and has as its aim a new whole taking into account new elements, and a set of ideas is true to the extent that the action called out by those ideas can be carried out under the existing circumstances. A false set of ideas is one which does not permit the resumption of the interrupted activity. A fully successful set of ideas becomes a mechanical habit, and as action becomes thus mechanical, thought ceases. Only as new obstacles or interruptions arise to make habit ineffective does thought re-enter. It is the task of logic to point out the reconstructive function of thought and to indicate how the reconstructive process provides the criteria of thought.

And, once more, from this logical theory of the act of thought all the branches of philosophy derive. A true conception of this as a philosophy requires, however, that the social nature of the logical theory be made clear. The thought process can come into being only in an organism that is in essential relations with other organisms in some systematic manner. Moore points out that the appearance of conflicts of the sort necessary for the birth of thought is dependent upon a social context. Habit, perception, memory are functions of interacting beings and do not belong exclusively to any of the individual beings involved.[69] Mead works out in elaborate detail the social basis of communication, meaning, and self-consciousness upon which this logic rests, but all the others of the Chicago School presuppose this basis in their thought.

Men's activities take many forms: automatic reactions, enjoyments, adorations, sufferings, thinkings. Thinking is a kind of action, not generically distinct from other kinds. But it is the most important kind, because in thought men attempt to control themselves and their environment. And all human problems are problems of control. This is the view of the world to which the Chicagoans insisted we must turn if thought is to be effective and meaningful in a world in which the results of men's activities are fast outrunning men's ability to control or even understand those results. Hence their criticisms of those intellectual schemes that left us trapped inside our world of mere ideas – whether those ideas were referred to atomic sensations or to Absolute Mind. As Mead said of Moore, it can be said of all the members of this philosophic movement: "He began his speculative thinking with a world which was there, a world that put up to our intelligence the precarious task of living within it, and he refused to arrest action in order to prove the existence of that world."[70] The insight of Locke and Hume that ultimately our knowledge of the reality of the world is a practical knowledge, that we know the world is real and that we are real because we can act in reference to the world with some consistency and coherence, was expanded into a genuine philosophy of the practical that brought thought once more into direct contact with the ordinary man's experience and provided the means for the growth of that experience into something more than ordinary.

III

PSYCHOLOGY · *Functionalism and Behaviorism*

THE new psychology developing in the United States and Germany appeared to offer a whole new method for inquiry. Formal logic, even in its new discoveries, was too remote from experience to serve in the role of method. Psychology, on the other hand, was allying itself with biology and physiology and adopting the experimental techniques and positivistic attitudes of those sciences; hence it held the promise of a more practical kind of logic. Dewey saw the possibilities in the new psychology of a natural account of mind and hence of experience: "In psychology this conception [organism] has led to the recognition of mental life as an organic unitary process developing according to the laws of all life, and not a theatre for the exhibition of independent autonomous faculties, or a *rendezvous* in which isolated, atomic sensations and ideas may gather, hold external converse, and then forever part. . . . The idea of environment is a necessity to the idea of organism, and with the conception of environment comes the impossibility of considering psychical life as an individual, isolated thing developing in a vacuum."[1]

However, Dewey had only begun to move toward a biological conception of mind. As late as 1886, he was still talking of a universal consciousness,[2] although he dropped the notion by the time he published his *Psychology* in 1887. In *Psychology*, universal consciousness was replaced by *knowledge* as the universal element or aspect of consciousness, while *emotion* is the individual element and *will* includes both. But even in the third edition he still wrote of the soul as a thing distinct from the body, with a mechanism of its own that was roused by changes in the nervous system but once roused acted in accordance with its own structure and produced within itself the unique activity we know as sensation.[3] This dualistic view remained in the third edition of *Psychology* (1891), even though he had in 1890 relegated the distinction between fact and idea to one which takes place "within and on account of the judgment — the logical process." [4]

Dewey credits James's *The Principles of Psychology* with having brought home to him the biological nature of mind, but he says that James himself made practically nothing of this conception.[5] Dewey's 1896 article, "The Reflex Arc Concept in Psychology," is widely credited as the foundation of functional psychology as a distinct movement. There were earlier statements indicative of what was to be distinctive about functionalism, however. In his article "Herr Lasswitz on Energy and Epistemology," Mead pointed to the continuity of physics and psychology: "If, now, the psychological object be formed out of full sensuous activities responding to stimuli which affect the different sense-organs; if these reactions take place in a system built up by action upon its environment, and if the relations of its environment to it are expressed in the fundamental laws of energy, evidently those reactions and those objects must be functions of the laws of physics." [6] Psychological activities can be interpreted as processes in relation to biological or physical processes — e.g., the food-process or energy exchange. (Mead points out, however, that efforts to parallel psychology and physics have not altogether succeeded.)

Dewey had also developed his functional theory of emotion in the *Psychological Review* in 1894 and 1895, making such characteristic statements as the following:

. . . we work in a wrong, a hopeless direction when we start from the emotion and attempt to derive the movements as its expression; while the situation clears itself up when we start from the character of the movement, as a completed or disturbed coordination, and then derive the corresponding types of normal and pathological emotion.[7]

. . . *the mode of behavior is the primary thing, and . . . the idea and the emotional excitation are constituted at one and the same time . . . indeed, they represent the tension of stimulus and response within the coordination which makes up the mode of behavior.*

. . . this distinction of 'object' and 'response' is one of interpretation, or value, and not a plain matter of course difference in the experiencing.[8]

The first of the "Studies from the Psychological Laboratory of the University of Chicago" appeared in 1896. "Reaction-Time: A Study in Attention and Habit" by Angell and Moore states in experimental terms the position stated theoretically by the subsequent "Reflex Arc Concept." In summing up their observations of the relation between the ear and the hand in a response test, Angell and Moore assert a basic functionalist tenet:

The hand therefore is stimulus as well as response to the ear, and the latter is response as well as stimulus to the hand. . . . The distinction of stimulus and response is therefore not one of *content* . . . but one of *function*, and both offices belong equally to each organ. . . . the entire act is the act of attention in coordinating the two groups of stimuli coming from both hand and ear. To be sure, *in* the act of coordination there is, as we have seen, the interaction of the two elements as stimulus and response each to the other. But it must be kept in mind that this latter is a distinction falling *inside* the act, not *between* the hand movement considered as the act, and the sound considered as its external stimulus or 'cause.' In a word, the reagent reacts as much with his ear as he does with his hand.[9]

Angell and Moore credit this interpretation of the experiment to suggestions from Dewey and Mead; and Dewey acknowledges that several of the key ideas in his translation of Darwin's theory of emotion into a functional theory are due to Mead.[10] Mead's role is already discernible: involved intimately in all the researches going on, a fertile source of ideas, yet publishing comparatively little. Dewey is also developing his ideas rapidly and publishing the results almost as rapidly. Angell and Moore are testing and expanding upon ideas that seem to come primarily from Mead and Dewey.* Tufts does not appear to be directly involved in the psychology laboratory, since his interests remain social and the laboratory concerns were not social.

"The Reflex Arc Concept" remains the most significant single statement of functional psychology, however. It was in this article that Dewey launched his most direct attack on dualism and laid the basis for a process theory of mental activity. It opens with a comparison of the current dualism of stimulus and response to the older dualism of sensation and idea or body and soul. Without explicit announcement,† Dewey is formally rejecting his earlier views and setting forth a naturalism that excludes any transcendental element in the explanation of man's experience. His objection to the reflex arc concept (previously voiced in the Angell and Moore study) is that the sensory stimulus, the central activity (the idea), and the motor discharge are treated as three distinct things, with no intelligible connections. He regards the three as functions within the act, not as distinct parts but as distinctions of interpretation unified within the coordination of movement. As he points out, the key to his conception of psychological activity is coordination.

The analysis of the act that was to be fundamental to the new

* Angell, in his autobiographical essay in *A History of Psychology in Autobiography*, ed. Carl Murchison, Vol. 3 (Worcester, Mass.: Clark University Press, 1936), remarks about the reflex arc article that "The article incorporated one of Dewey's flashes of insight which in other hands would perhaps have been more patiently developed and consequently led to more fruitful consequences in the area outside the Chicago group" (p. 25). Angell gives due credit to Dewey and Moore for their work in psychology and mentions Mead and Tufts, but he is concerned in retrospect to claim his work as his own and to explain the failure of functional psychology as a continuing force of major proportions.

† In the second article on emotion, Dewey refers in a note to his view in his *Psychology* that feeling is the internalization of activity or will, and he credits James with furnishing "this old idealistic conception of feeling, hitherto blank and unmediated, with a medium of translation into the terms of concrete phenomena." *Psychological Review*, 2 (no. 1): 15 (January 1895). There is an interesting addition to this note: "On the historical side, it may be worth noting that a crude anticipation of James's theory is found in Hegel's *Philosophie des Geistes*, §401."

experimental logic here yields a two-stage teleological process. The first is that of a realized adaptation; an act always proceeds out of a prior coordination, a habit, or an instinct, in which stimulus and response, means and end are completely integrated. Because distinctions such as stimulus and response or means and end are useful for interpreting the formation of this coordination, we read them into the coordination as separate elements, whereas they are thoroughly integrated and organized in the habitual act. The second stage occurs when a problematic situation arises. The habitual act no longer serves; the response is uncertain—and so is the stimulus. In fact, the real problem is that of what sort of stimulus is present, not that of what sort of response is called for by a definite stimulus. The stimulus must be determined before a significant response can take place. In the case of the child and the burning candle, once he has been burned, the child has a problem when presented with a bright light. Sometimes a bright thing has been a beautiful plaything, sometimes a thing that burns. The problem is, what sort of light is this?

A sensation, then, is not a separate existence but a phase of some coordination that requires attention because of the problem present. The act, Dewey says, that was objective stimulus in the previous condition of coordination is transformed into a sensation as a possible stimulus, and motion as conscious response emerges. The subjective element comes to be because there is an interruption in the smooth ongoing of the act. The sensation, therefore, instead of being a given element out of which the activities of the mind are built, is a phase of the act whose particular nature must be accounted for in terms of the kind of activity within which it appears.*

Correspondingly, motion or response is a functional aspect of the

* Note the same point of view as it occurs in Angell's statements about consciousness in his *Psychology* (New York: Henry Holt): "If the reflexes and the automatic acts were wholly competent to steer the organism throughout its course, there is no reason to suppose that consciousness would ever put in an appearance" (1st ed., 1904, p. 50; 4th ed., 1908, p. 64) and ". . . it may be asserted that consciousness in one or other of its forms normally appears and participates only in such activities as cannot be efficiently executed by the hereditary reflexes and the acquired automatisms" (4th ed., p. 63).

problematic stage of action. The response is whatever occurs as a possible means of reinstatement of the interrupted coordination; it is the potential solution of the problem marked by the sensation or stimulus. There is no such thing, on this view, as a stimulus or a response as a thing in itself. What is a stimulus under one set of conditions may be a response under another set, and vice versa. The whole process is unified by the concept of the coordination, an organic circuit rather than a reflex arc.

Perhaps the most important aspect of this theory for psychology was the shift from concern with the structure of the mind to concern with the functions of the mind. A structural approach necessitated conceiving of the mind as a thing composed of elements, hence as distinct from the body. The structuralists generally accepted the notion of psychophysical parallelism and tried to ignore the mind-body problem as far as possible.* Functionalism avoided the mind-body problem by treating mental activities as particular kinds of functions of the organism in its interactions with its environment. The functionalists still dealt with consciousness, but consciousness was a phase of problem-solving activity of the organism and not a manifestation of a nonphysical entity such as mind or soul had formerly been considered. The decisive change was from a psychology of entities to a psychology of process. Angell wrote: "The position to which I refer [functionalism] regards the mind-body relation as capable of treatment in psychology as a methodological distinction rather than a metaphysically existential one." [11]

Titchener was quick to seize upon what appeared to be two vulnerable spots in functionalism: its teleological leanings and its connection with philosophy. To him, both aspects were unscientific, and nothing was calculated to damn a psychological theory as thoroughly as the charge of being unscientific:

There is, further, the danger that, if function is studied before structure has been fully elucidated, the student may fall into that

* E. B. Titchener and his followers were the principal representatives of structural psychology in the period in which the Chicago group was developing.

acceptance of teleological explanation which is fatal to scientific advance: witness, if witness be necessary, the recrudescence of vitalism in physiology. Psychology might thus put herself for the second time, and no less surely though by different means, under the dominion of philosophy. In a word, the historical conditions of psychology rendered it inevitable that, when the time came for the transformation from philosophy to science, problems should be formulated, explicitly or implicitly, as static rather than dynamic, structural rather than functional.[12]

Angell's statements about the connections between functional psychology and logic, ethics, and aesthetics (quoted in Chapter II on pages 29–30) gave Titchener further evidence of the unscientific (and nonpsychological) nature of functionalism:

Introspection, from the structural standpoint, is an observation of an Is; introspection, from the functional standpoint, is observation of an Is-for. Unschooled introspection tends almost irresistibly, then, to the introspection of an Is-for. But there are two extra-psychological functions that we are very apt to appeal to, in mental reference: the Is-for-thought and the Is-for-conduct. In other words, unschooled introspection is apt to be an introspection, not of psychological material at all, but of meanings (logical function) or of values (ethical function).[13]

The Chicago group was not frightened at the connection between philosophy and psychology, however. Mead, as we have seen, expanded what Dewey had to say about the continuity of the stimulus-response situation into a program for philosophy. He also extrapolated Dewey's reflex arc idea into a theory of the psychical.[14] In this essay, Mead objects to attempts to account for the psychical phase of experience by converting objects *in toto* into ideas or by taking whatever is left over from a scientific analysis of an object and relegating it to the psychical. In both cases, what is subjective is the idea or image or quality *of* something; hence it is not immediate in the sense that subjective consciousness always is. In the psychical situation the object has disintegrated and has to be reconstructed out of the conditions presented by the problem that led to the disintegration. The psychical, then, is the activity of this reconstruction. Mead defines the subject matter of functional psychology as "that phase of experience within which we are immediately conscious of conflicting impulses which rob the object of its character as object-stimulus, leaving us in so far in an attitude of subjectivity; but during which a new object-stimulus appears due to the reconstructive activity which is identified with the subject 'I' as distinct from the object 'me.'"[15] He thus restores the "loss of dignity of content" of the "I" by making the subject (the psychical) an activity, a function necessarily involved in moving from a coordination through a disintegration to a new coordination. There is no mind-body distinction in the subjective stage, any more than there is in a complete coordination. There is no object in the subjective phase; there is only what James calls the stream of consciousness. Mead calls the reconstructive activity the individual:

What I wish to insist upon is that, while we have not as yet a predicate, we also have no subject; that, while the negative statement of the problem clears the ground for its solution, it does not give that solution; and that the statement of the rest of experience in terms of the conditions of the solution of the problem, the gathering of data, does not give the positive touch of reconstruction which is involved in the presentation of a hypothesis, however slight and vague it may be; that this step takes place within the field of subjectivity, which in so far is neither me nor other, neither mind nor body. And it is in this phase of subjectivity, with its activities of attention in the solution of the problem, i.e., in the construction of the hypothesis of the new world, that the individual *qua* individual has his functional expression or rather is that function.[16]

The science of psychology has, then, as its concern, according to Mead, the description and definition of the subjective phase of consciousness: "the statement of the conflict of an impulse with a co-ordination of impulses and the inhibition of these impulses" and of "the shifting of attention in the reco-ordination of these impulses, the control of the outgoing activities by the sense-processes during this co-ordination, and the like."[17] Psychology has to deal with the various kinds of subjectivity in terms of the processes whose laws would be stated by logic. This means that all psychical phenomena must be accounted for as arising out of problem-solving activity. So long as activity moves smoothly by instinct or habit, there is no psychic phase; but all the immediate awareness we have of feelings, emotions, images, ideas, and mental constructions comes into being when the instinctual or habitual reaction no longer serves our ends.

The intellectual aspect of consciousness nowhere receives what Mead would call a psychological analysis. It gets a full-scale treatment in logical analysis by Dewey, Moore, and Tufts. And Angell presupposes the logical studies of the appearance of consciousness in his *Psychology*, but he only gives a statement of the conditions and not a psychological analysis of the process.

Dewey's theory of emotion previously mentioned does provide an example of the sort of psychological analysis Mead indicated. Dewey disagrees with both Darwin and James on emotion. In the first place, he says that emotions cannot be accounted for as expressions of something, as Darwin treats them. A viewer interprets the emotion of an animal as expressive, but for the animal the emotion is part of the act or movement in which it is engaged. The animal is *acting*, not expressing a feeling or an attitude.* Emotions are attitudes deriving from purposive acts – whether or not those attitudes still serve the original end. In Dewey's words, "the principle of explanation *actually* used, whatever the form of words employed, is that of survival, in the form of attitudes, of acts originally useful not *qua* expressing emotion, but *qua* acts – as serving life." [18] Emotional discharges are disturbances of adjusted movements; those discharges which are not adjusted movements or disturbances of such movements have no emotional quality. His example is that of trembling with cold as opposed to trembling with rage or fear. The latter is emotional, the former is not.

In the second place, James fails, according to Dewey, to connect emotional seizure with the whole situation of having an emotion. In saying that we are sad because we cry, James has called attention to the function of the organism in emotion, but he has merely reversed the traditional causal order and has not really *explained*

* Dewey uses this same basic argument forty-five years later against A. J. Ayer's theory that value expressions are merely ejaculatory. *Theory of Valuation* (Chicago: University of Chicago Press, 1939), pp. 8–9.

emotion. For Dewey, the explanation lies in the whole concrete emotional experience. This experience has three phases: (1) it is an affect or seizure; (2) it is a mode of conduct; and (3) it is always "about" or "toward" something – it has an object and hence an intellectual content. The emotional aspect of this situation, Dewey says, "is, *psychologically, the adjustment or tension of habit and ideal*, and the organic changes in the body are the literal working out, in concrete terms, of the struggle of adjustment." [19] The attitude was once a complete activity but is no longer. It is now an inhibited activity which plays its part within a larger activity as a reinforcing or checking factor. The conflict of attitudes in such a complex situation is the emotional disturbance. The original activity that is now an attitude and now gives rise to emotion from its inhibition probably had no emotional quality in its more primitive exstence. So emotion, on this view, is not simply the result of an organic disturbance; rather, it is the product of a condition of tension or conflict, the resolution of which involves bodily changes as well as emotional states. (In all the editions of his *Psychology*, Angell adopted Dewey's theory of emotion with almost no qualification, although he does not mention Dewey's modifications of Darwin's theory of emotion in his "The Influence of Darwin on Psychology." [20] And in *An Introduction to Psychology*, he merely refers to Dewey's theory along with those of James-Lange, Darwin, and Watson.[21] When Harvey Carr wrote his *Psychology*,[22] his discussion of emotion was closer to Watson's theory than Dewey's, and neither Dewey nor Mead is mentioned in the book.)

The same kind of analysis holds for sensation, images, ideas, interests, and motives. Consciousness, in whatever form, emerges from an interruption in some ongoing process.[23] A sensation is not just a stimulus; it is an act, an act of seeing, hearing, smelling that involves muscular response as well as sensory stimulus. A sensation is the aspect of a coordination that first comes to conscious attention because of a conflict within the coordination: the sensation is a possible stimulus in the face of an uncertainty. The particular quality of a sensation depends upon the nature of the process out of which it arises and upon how it is being used to reinstate that process.[24]

Dewey made no more such basic analyses as this after "The Reflex Arc Concept." His interest in psychology, after the *Psychology*, was in the bearings of psychology on logic, ethics, and education. He made no claim to be a psychologist; he knew that psychology had moved into the laboratory and had become specialized to the point that, as a philosopher, he could only try to keep up with developments relevant to his philosophic interests. In a letter to Arthur Bentley in 1935, Dewey states this point explicitly: "I do not pretend to be a psychologist anyway, and what I've written on that subject has been mostly for the sake of clearing up my own mind about something in either ethics or logic: consequently I'm aware that it is not systematic and probably not even self-consistent."[25] He did, of course, continue to concern himself with the bearings of psychology on education and on ethics. And in 1930 Dewey still saw a validity in his original conception of a stimulus, as opposed to that of the structuralists he was reacting against at the time and that of the behaviorists who took the field against functionalism:

> The basic error of the structuralists was, it seems to me, the assumption that the phenomena they dealt with had a structure which direct inspection could disclose. Admitting, for the moment, that there are such things as conscious processes which constitute "experience" and which are capable of direct inspection, it still involves an immense leap of logic to infer that direct inspection can disclose their structures. One might go so far as to say that, supposing that there are such things, they are just the sort of things that are, in their immediate occurrence, structureless. Or, to put it in a more exact way, if they have any structure, this is not carried in their immediate presence but in facts that are external to them and which cannot be disclosed by the method of direct inspection.
>
> It seems to me that there is considerable behavioristic and semi-behavioristic theory in psychology at present that is content merely to subsume the phenomena in question under the rubric of S-R as if they were ready-made and self-evident things.
>
> When we turn to the consideration of *what* is a stimulus, we ob-

tain a result which is fatal to the idea that isolated acts, typified by a reflex, can be used to determine the meaning of stimulus. That which is, or operates as, a stimulus turns out to be a function, in a mathematical sense, of behavior in its serial character. Something, not yet a stimulus, breaks in upon an activity already going on and *becomes* a stimulus in virtue of the relations it sustains to what is going on in this continuing activity. . . . One and the same environmental change becomes, under different conditions of ongoing or serial behavior, a thousand different actual stimuli—a consideration which is fatal to the supposition that we can analyze behavior into a succession of independent stimuli and responses. . . . A stimulus is always a *change* in the environment which is connected with a *change* in activity. No stimulus is a stimulus to action as such but only to a change in the direction or intensity of action. A response is not action or behavior but marks a change in behavior.[26]

The separation of philosophy and psychology discussed at the beginning of the previous chapter was important for psychology, as it was for philosophy at Chicago. Functional psychology continued as a school under Angell and later under Carr. But the distinctive concepts of functionalism had been worked out by the philosophers, and once the psychology was removed from its intellectual sources, it did not have the impetus for the kind of growth necessary for such a school to remain a major force in a rapidly growing field. Angell's writings contain little of original theoretical content, and his laboratory experiments did not long continue to turn up data of importance to the rest of his profession. Shortly after he became chairman of the Department of Psychology at Chicago, Angell moved into administrative work in the university. In 1920 he became president of the Carnegie Corporation, and almost immediately thereafter, president of Yale University. In his autobiographical article in *A History of Psychology in Autobiography*, Angell says that he was introduced to psychology by Dewey's textbook on the subject, but he found James's *Principles of Psychology* more stimulating.[27] He sees Dewey, James, and Darwin as the central influences on his own ideas, and the statements he makes on functionalism in 1936 sound much like the statements he, Dewey, and Mead were making forty years earlier. Angell mentions among his contributions to psychology the experiment on reaction time he did with Moore, an experiment with Simon F. McLennan on the organic effects of pleasure and pain [28] which was inconclusive, an experiment with Helen B. Thompson on the organic accompaniments of conscious processes,[29] and his experiments on the significance of partial tones for the localization of sound.[30]

John Broadus Watson became Angell's assistant in 1902 and was named instructor in experimental psychology in 1904. Watson was evidently the man chosen to move into the lead in the experimental work at Chicago, although he points out that Dewey and Angell both told him that his graduate work was inferior to that of Miss Thompson. Watson recalls his whole career at Chicago with a mixture of fondness and bitterness. He had gone to Chicago for graduate study because of Dewey, but his interests quickly shifted from philosophy to psychology, and his major work there was done with Angell, Donaldson in neurology, and Loeb in physiology. Of his philosophy courses at Chicago, Watson said:

God knows I took enough philosophy to know something about it. But it wouldn't take hold. I passed my exams but the spark was not there. I got something out of the British School of Philosophers—mainly out of Hume, a little out of Locke, a bit out of Hartley, nothing out of Kant, and, strange to say, least of all out of John Dewey. I never knew what he was talking about then, and, unfortunately for me, I still don't know. Tufts and Moore were patient with me and I attach no blame to them for my failing to flower in philosophy. I took courses and seminars with Mead. I didn't understand him in the classroom, but for years Mead took a great interest in my animal experimentation, and many a Sunday he and I spent in the laboratory watching my rats and monkeys. On these comradely exhibitions and at his home I understood him. A kinder, finer man I never met.[31]

It is evident from these remarks on his reactions to the philosophers at Chicago why Watson did not turn out to be the heir to functionalism. Although he did not set forth his brand of behaviorism publicly until after he went to Johns Hopkins in 1908, his mechanistic views already had been shaped, primarily by Loeb, with whom he had wanted to do his thesis research. But, as he says, "Neither Angell nor Donaldson in those days felt that Loeb was a very 'safe' man for a green Ph.D. candidate." [32] Watson dates his first "conversational formulation" of behaviorism to 1903, but adds that the formulation was not encouraged.[33] Angell wrote a paper critical of what he called the excesses of behaviorism in 1913.[34] Watson's denial of the reality as well as usefulness of such concepts as consciousness, sensation, perception, desire, purpose, and the like made him something of a scandal in academic circles and cut him off from the school out of which he came. Watson's divorce from his wife in 1920 was accompanied by sufficient public attention that he was forced to resign from Johns Hopkins, and he left the academic world for good (except for later lectures at the New School) to begin a successful career in advertising. Watson's bitterness about his whole university experience came not just from the scandal but from the reactions of some of his former teachers and colleagues to his later writings and activities. He mentions in particular the criticism of him by Angell, then president of Yale, in a commencement address at Dartmouth.[35] Certainly, Watson is the most spectacular product of the Chicago School of Psychology. He is one of several who became well known but not as functional psychologists – among them, Jacob R. Kantor, Beardsley Ruml, and L. L. Thurstone. Watson did not endear himself to Angell and others by his continuing disparagement of functionalism as a timid behaviorism: "Most of the younger psychologists realize that some such formulation as behaviorism is the only road leading to science. Functional psychology cannot help. It died of its own half-heartedness before behaviorism was born." [36]

Harvey Carr continued the tradition in psychology at Chicago – and ended it. He went to Chicago in 1902, where he found himself with a fellowship in education, much to his dismay. He took the usual courses in philosophy, reporting that Plato, Kant, Locke, and Berkeley made the most impression on him. The contrast of his reaction to the philosophers with that of Watson's indicates a difference in turn of mind reflected in their respective psychologies. But Carr also took a course in experimental psychology with

Angell that first year and found his future course set. Dewey left shortly after Carr arrived at Chicago, and Carr worked principally with Angell and Watson. Again in contrast to Watson, Carr found Donaldson's work in neurology admirable but not a source of enthusiasm. After he got his degree in 1905, he taught in a Texas high school and then at Pratt Institute. In 1908 he returned to Chicago to take Watson's place. Carr continued Watson's laboratory work with animals, and he was involved in a number of experiments in learning. But he reports that he early saw the limitations on laboratory experiments with human beings, and in the pragmatic spirit of the Chicago School, he could not turn exclusively to non-human concerns in psychology. And Carr never was obsessed with making psychology a science. He looked upon science with the kind of openness Dewey and Mead showed:

I am skeptical of the attempt to define science on the basis of its subject matter. Is psychology a science? I have never been interested in the question. It makes no difference to me. Science is primarily a matter of attitude and method. The important question, to my mind, is: Are psychologists scientists? And I think that most of them are – at times – just like physicists and chemists. Perhaps the essence of the method is the spirit and not the form of the inquiry, and again I shall not define these terms. I am inclined to believe that the form of attack will necessarily vary with the problem, and that in time we will devise modes of attack adapted to psychological problems which at present are not subject to scientific investigation.[37]

Despite the influence that Watson did have on psychology, the functionalists did not really relinquish their concern with consciousness, which Watson considered in the same category as soul. By the time functional psychology was beginning to take form, the term "soul" was in bad repute in the field, and "mind" was becoming questionable. In Angell's *Psychology*, psychology is defined as the science of consciousness, and both soul and mind are rejected as the subject matter of the discipline, soul because of its supernatural connotations and mind because it is too narrow for the total concern of psychology. The same concept of psychology appears in Angell's *Chapters from Modern Psychology*.[38] But when his *Introduction* appeared (1918), he pointed out that the term "consciousness" had joined "soul" and "mind" in general disfavor in his profession, and he went along with the trend to the extent of accepting the definition that psychology is the science of behavior. But he insisted that behavior is to include thinking, feeling, and acting, whereas the "pure behaviorist" would disregard thinking and feeling. These changes in terminology indicate the intermediate position functionalism occupies between the old psychologies of the soul and the more recent psychologies of external activity. In 1925, Carr still maintained that "Psychology is primarily concerned with the study of mental activity. This term is the generic name for such activities as perception, memory, imagination, reasoning, feeling, judgment, and will." [39]

In his book, Carr appears almost to have gone back to the concept of the reflex arc that Dewey had rejected in his early statement of the principles of functionalism. He talks of the nervous system as a means of translating sensory stimuli into movements that are adaptive in character. But he is not just reasserting the doctrine of stimuli and response as fixed distinctions—although he is closer to that doctrine than Dewey and Angell were. He names three general principles derivable from his conception of the role of the nervous system: (1) "All sensory stimuli must exert some effect upon the activity of the organism. Any stimulating condition that affects a sense organ necessarily releases energy, and the only outlet for this energy is the muscles and glands." [40] (2) "All activity, ideational as well as motor, is initiated by sensory stimuli. The sensory-neuro-muscular mechanisms accumulate and store energy, and this energy can be released only by the incidence of extraneous forces upon the sensitive parts." [41] (3) "Every movement resulting from a sensory situation inevitably modifies that situation, and this change or modification of the sensory situation constitutes a new sensory stimulus which in turn modifies the act that produced it. There is thus a continuous process of interaction between sensory stimuli and motor responses." [42] His concern with the adaptation of the organism *to* the environment is closer to Darwin than Dewey ever was. This is probably due more to Watson and some of the other behaviorists than to Darwin, however. There is still present in Carr's outlook the broader concern with the whole situation within which an act occurs and with the interaction between organism and environment: "Any adaptive act is always performed in the presence of a wider sensory environment, and all aspects of this sensory situation will affect the organism and release nervous impulses that must find a motor outlet. Any adaptive response to an object must thus be influenced by and be dependent upon the entire sensory situation of the moment. We may thus say that an organism reacts to the sensory situation as a whole while it adapts to or reacts toward but one aspect of that situation." [43]

Charles H. Judd is frequently classified as one of the Chicago functionalists, and he was. He arrived at his position independently of the Chicago School, however. Judd studied with Wilhelm Wundt at Leipzig, but developed from the Wundtian perspective a remarkably close parallel to the Chicago functionalism, and he shared with Mead a high regard for the social psychology in Wundt's *Völkerpsychologie*, which was generally neglected at the time by American psychologists. After teaching at New York University, the University of Cincinnati, and Yale, Judd went to Chicago in 1909 as director of the School of Education. Two years before, he had published his *Psychology*, in which he said, "This book aims to develop a functional view of mental life. Indeed, I am quite unable to accept the contentions, or sympathize with the views of the defenders of a structural or purely analytical psychology." [44] None of the Chicago psychologists or philosophers is taken account of in the book, but there are passages that could be attributed to Dewey or Mead or Angell without distortion. For example, compare the following with Dewey's views discussed on page 60: "It will be seen that the sensory, central, and motor processes cannot be sharply distinguished from each other; they are all phases of a single continuous process, the end of which is always some muscular activity." [45] "The function which a given sensation serves is not determined merely by the quality or intensity of the sensation; it is determined in large measure by the relation into which the sensation enters." [46] Chapters VI and VII ("Sensations and Their

Functional Relations" and "Experience and Expression") are overtly functional in their analyses, as Judd emphasizes at the end of Chapter VII:

The analysis of experience which has been worked out in the last two chapters is distinctly functional in type. There is a disposition in some quarters to reduce feeling and attention, and the other phases of experience, to elements, and to regard them as "structural" rather than "functional" phases of experience. Such reduction of all experience to a common "structural" character makes it very difficult to find any physiological formulas for the conditions of these complex processes of arrangement, and sacrifices the complexity of real experience in the interests of simplicity and uniformity of description.[47]

Judd's interest in the social dimensions of psychology, as evidenced in the chapter on language in *Psychology* and later in his *The Psychology of Social Institutions*[48] and his *Educational Psychology*,[49] was closer to the spirit of functionalism (at least, according to Mead) than to the narrower concepts of the functionalists in the Department of Psychology (see below, page 77).

But there is no indication in the writings of Judd or of the various members of the Chicago School that there was any direct interchange between the School and Judd. Tufts refers to Judd twice in his book *America's Social Morality*,[50] but only in quoting statistics from a report to which Judd had contributed. Judd provides grounds for the contention that functionalism was in the air at the time and in some cases was the result of a variety of indirect factors rather than just of the direct influence of any man or men.

Functional psychology has left no direct descendants, which should not be surprising in as rapidly evolving a field as psychology is. Its influence has spread in several directions, that of behaviorism and that of some reactions to the extremes of behaviorism. Edna Heidbreder says that behaviorism and Gestalt psychology pushed functionalism aside, but she also says that functionalism was a major factor in turning American psychology away from structures and faculties to action:

To study functions is to study activities that are connected with the world at both ends, activities which typically are initiated by external stimuli and which terminate in operations on the external world. Thus the outstanding contribution of functionalism is its conception of psychological processes not as something remote and detached, but as rooted in the conditions in which they are actually found; effective in the sense that other biological activities are effective, making some difference in the world by their operations, not merely reflecting or keeping step with the procession of events they accompany.[51]

One factor that should be mentioned in passing is the lack of influence of psychoanalysis on functionalism. Like most traditional psychologists in the United States, the functionalists have ignored or scorned the psychoanalysts. Dewey takes a passing notice of them in *Human Nature and Conduct*[52] and in *The Sources of a Science of Education*,[53] but Angell puts his opposition clearly: "Despite my early and sincere interest in abnormal psychology, the Freudian movement with its sundry variants found me driven into an attitude of criticism and hostility, for, while I regarded certain of its contributions as sound and fundamentally significant, not a little appeared to be somewhat romantic and distinctly unscientific. The excesses of its proponents, many of them psychiatrists of the slenderest scientific equipment, compelled me to adopt a position of rather active opposition."[54] And although he gives a brief statement of Freud's theory of dreams in his *Introduction*,[55] Angell does not discuss Freud or psychoanalysis. In this connection, it is interesting to note the reason Angell gives for not discussing sex in his *Psychology*: "The delineation of the basal facts in the birth and development of love between the sexes has been accomplished so perfectly in the great poems and tales of passion as to render futile and superfluous any such brief outline as would be possible here."[56] Sex is not mentioned in his *Introduction*, and any discussion of the role of sex in psychological development (apart from mention of mating behavior of the male pigeon) is notably absent from Carr's book. Of course, it should be said that, during the first quarter of this century, an author of a textbook had to be very careful to avoid anything that might conceivably smack of sensationalism. Even the indomitable Watson felt this restriction on him: "Another reason which deters me from enlarging upon this aspect of psychology is that the discussion of total activity [of the totally integrated individual] involves a frankness in dealing with human nature which the American school public is not yet educated to entertain." [57] But Carr also shared Angell's attitude toward psychoanalysis: "Like most psychologists, I am extremely skeptical of much of the subterranean mental machinery of the psychoanalysts. Nevertheless the problem is still there, for what we write and the manner thereof – especially in an article such as this – is an expression of our nature and may reveal much. But which of the various interpretations is correct? Such questions can hardly be decided on the basis of present techniques." [58] Watson, as might be expected, was less circumspect. In arguing that behaviorism is the only path to science for psychology, he says: "Freudianism cannot help. Where it is more than a technique it is an emotional defense of a hero. It can never serve as a support for a scientific formulation." [59]

There was one deviation from traditional psychology that became important at Chicago, however. Although Dewey early distinguished psychology as individual from sociology as social,[60] neither he nor others in his department considered psychology as purely individual. Individual psychological processes are social; the psychologist simply looks at them from the standpoint of the individual processes. And the need for a social dimension to psychology is continually recognized by the Chicago philosophers. Tufts wrote: "There is no 'individual mind,' i.e., mind not under the constant influence of the social relations; neither can we hope to find any 'social' knowledge or feeling, i.e., knowledge or feeling not existing in the medium of individual consciousness. We may doubtless study various aspects of consciousness in isolation, but their abstract character should be distinctly recognized, and neither 'psychologist' nor 'sociologist' can ignore the work of the other." [61] Dewey commented: "Psychology is the attempt to state in detail the machinery of the individual considered as the instrument and organ through which social action operates." [62] But Mead developed a peculiarly social psychology, as distinct from individual psychology and with a more specific province than sociology, and he stated the basis of this psychology as early as 1895: "We are as essentially social beings as physical and physiological beings, despite the analogy of the clocks. . . . The development of the distinction between the physical and psychical in others proceeds *pari passu* with that in the child's consciousness of himself – if for no other reason because he could never form the conception of himself as psychical without the conception of others. Or again man is essentially social." [63]

Mead's social psychology was touched upon in the last chapter, but it warrants some further remarks here. Mead viewed the developments of functional psychology as definitely an improvement over structural approaches, but what he came to see as its individualistic bent made it ultimately unsatisfactory:

The molecular structure of things seemed to remove these [secondary qualities] from the hypothetical objects of physical science, and consciousness proved a welcome dumping-ground for them. . . . Psychology, however, has not been interested in these epistemological and metaphysical riddles, it has been simply irritated by them. It has shifted its interest to the processes, where phenomenalism is most harmless, appearing as physiological psychology, as functional psychology, as dynamic psychology, and has ignored the problems for which it had no care. The effect of this has been to give the central nervous system a logical pre-eminence in the procedure and textbooks of psychology which is utterly unwarranted in the analysis of the experience of the individual. The central nervous system has been unwittingly assimilated to the logical position of consciousness. It occupies only an important stage in the act, but we find ourselves locating the whole environment of the individual in its convolutions. It is small wonder, then, that behaviorism has been welcomed with unmistakable relief, for it has studied the conduct of animals in necessary ignoration of consciousness, and it has been occupied with the act as a whole, not as a nervous arc.[64]

The physiological emphasis in psychology inevitably led to a concentration on the individual organism rather than on the act situation from which functionalism originally derived its concepts and method. Mead remarks in 1909 [65] that the last chapter of Angell's *Psychology* deals with the sociality of the self and that the whole book would have a new meaning if reread in the light of that last chapter.*

In the same article,[66] Mead calls attention to three implications for psychology which he attributes respectively to McDougall, Royce, and Baldwin: (1) that human nature is endowed with and organized by social instincts and impulses; (2) that the consciousness of meaning has arisen through social intercommunication; and (3) that the self that is implied in every act with reference to which our primary judgments of valuation are made must exist in a social consciousness within which other selves are as immediately given as is the subject self.† Mead goes on to develop the further implications of these points.[67] The first implies (a) that the matter and form of social objects are implicit in man and (b) that what we call imitation can be explained as the same kind of tendencies or instincts in the young form being called out by the same or similar stimuli as call out the tendencies in the adults around him.‡ The second means that before reflective consciousness comes into being there must be social interactions involving gestures which are transformed into meanings when an individual uses a gesture in awareness of its value to others in the interaction. And the third states that other selves have to exist before one's own self can be defined; that a social group must exist as a condition for the emergence of self-consciousness.§

* In the fourth edition of *Psychology*, Angell uses Mead's terminology of the "me" side of consciousness in his discussion of the internal and external aspects of consciousness in the chapter on the self (p. 443). He had called this aspect simply the objective side in earlier editions.

† In an essay called "On Moral Evolution" in *Studies in Philosophy and Psychology* by former students of Charles Edward Garman (Boston: Houghton Mifflin, 1906), p. 3, Tufts listed three conceptions from psychology as important for explaining the moral life: (1) mental development starts with certain instincts and impulses, and intelligence arises largely from the blocking of the simple discharge of these impulses; (2) the self is many before it is one; and (3) the self is always a socius, in that other persons must be recognized before the self comes into being. Tufts maintained an interest in social psychology for its bearings on moral and social problems.

‡ This argument against the theory of imitation as the source of socialization remained basic for Mead. See *Mind, Self and Society* (Chicago: University of Chicago Press, 1934), pp. 58–61. There is imitation among higher animal forms but it is subsequent to more fundamental kinds of socialization.

§ Angell, in the chapter of his *Psychology* referred to above, says that the

Mead welcomed Watson's behaviorism because it was a move in the right direction: that of dealing with psychology in terms of action. The school of functional psychology, to which Mead was so close in the beginning, had moved in another direction so far that he lost interest in it. Of course, Watson's formulation of behaviorism was not adequate as the basis for a social psychology, and Mead pointed out that a psychology cannot merely abolish or ignore consciousness. Whatever else is or is not included in psychology, those phenomena which are accessible to the individual alone constitute that peculiar province of psychology.[68] What Mead proposes is to deal with both the inner and the outer sides of behavior in behavioristic terms:

> Social psychology is behavioristic in the sense of starting off with an observable activity — the dynamic, on-going social process, and the social acts which are its component elements — to be studied and analyzed scientifically. But it is not behavioristic in the sense of ignoring the inner experience of the individual — the inner phase of that process or activity. . . . It simply works from the outside to the inside instead of from the inside to the outside, so to speak, in its endeavor to determine how such experience does arise within the process. The act, then, and not the tract, is the fundamental datum in both social and individual psychology when behavioristically conceived, and it has both an inner and an outer phase, an internal and an external aspect.
>
> These general remarks have to do with our point of approach. It is behavioristic, but unlike Watsonian behaviorism it recognizes the parts of the act which do not come to external observation, and it emphasizes the act of the human individual in its natural social situation.[69]

In all probability, Watson's strong anti-philosophical bias, manifested in his claim to be unable to understand what either Dewey or Mead was talking about, was precisely his positivistic determination not to admit anything implied beyond or presupposed by

reply to the question whether a child growing up on a desert island would develop self-consciousness is that "undoubtedly something corresponding to self-consciousness might develop under such conditions through the operations of imagination" (1st ed., p. 389; 4th ed., p. 447). This seems a clear indication of Angell's individualism which moved Mead to call his own psychology behaviorism rather than functionalism.

that which is directly observable. This sort of bias precludes an explanation of anything, and that consequence is involved in Watson's prediction of the gradual disappearance of philosophy, it being replaced by the history of science.[70]

Mead's approach is exemplified by his discussion of the process by which animals acquire new reactions in his essay "Concerning Animal Perception."[71] He argues that plasticity in young animals is simply the existence of instinctive reactions in the animal which have not yet been called out by determinate external stimuli. The chick learns to reject the cinnabar caterpillar because its disagreeable taste calls forth the reaction of rejection in association with the perception peculiar to the caterpillar. This rejection further requires that distance perception be referred to contact experience. But this last statement has to do with an inner state of the chick, which cannot be observed directly by the psychologist (or, for that matter, by the chick either). Mead explains the fact of learning by the chick by analyzing the process into three stages: perception (usually visual), manipulation in contact experiences, and the culmination of the act (the actual eating, fighting, rejecting). These three stages were foreshadowed in Mead's analysis of the act of reflective thought.[72] There he found that the psychical stage of the act involves (1) a recognition of the reality of all the elements that enter into the experience; (2) conflicting tendencies to action asserting themselves; and (3) the resolution of the conflicts by a new tendency which leads to overt action or to an aesthetic representation. The same three stages appear as the stages of the act in *The Philosophy of the Act* with the prior stage of impulse (which appeared as the first of the implications for psychology referred to above, page 78) added to the stages of perception, manipulation, and consummation. The distinction between distance sensation and contact sensation was a fundamental one for Mead. It corresponds, of course, to Locke's distinction between secondary and primary qualities, a distinction much ridiculed from the standpoint of a variety of empiricisms. For Mead, it is a *practically* necessary distinction:

There is perhaps nothing inherent in contact experiences which accounts for their being the substantial element in perception—that to which, so far as physical, i.e., perceptual, experience goes, all other experience is referred. Visual discriminations are much finer and more accurate than those of manipulation. The auditory and olfactory experiences are richer in emotional valuations. But it remains true that our perception of physical objects always refers color, sound, odor, to a possibly handled substrate, a fact which was of course long ago recognized in the distinction between the so-called primary and secondary senses.

The ground of this is readily found in the nature of animal conduct, which, in so far as it is overt can be resolved into movements, stimulated by the distance senses, ending up in the attainment or avoidance of certain contacts.[73]

Not only do we explain animal conduct by this distinction, but human thought and consciousness as well. There can be symbols only where a distance perception refers to, means, or calls out habitual responses, tendencies to act, and possible contact sensations.

Within the framework provided by his analysis of the phases of the act, Mead proceeds to try to work out such psychological concepts as those of impulse, perception, thought, meaning, mind, and self. The psychology that results Mead considers true to the program of functional psychology in a way that the school of Angell and Carr was not; and from Mead's perspective, Watson's behaviorism was not so much a defection from functionalism as an aborted attempt to make good on the earlier promise of the Chicago psychology. Watson left out certain essentials for explaining the human individual; Angell got too far from the social context within which that individual was possible. As Mead said:

. . . the behavior of an individual can be understood only in terms of the behavior of the whole social group of which he is a member, since his individual acts are involved in larger, social acts which go beyond himself and which implicate the other members of that group. . . . For social psychology, the whole (society) is prior to the part (the individual), not the part to the whole; and the part is explained in terms of the whole, not the whole in terms of the part or parts. The social act is not explained by building it up out of stimulus plus response; it must be taken as a dynamic whole—as something going on—no part of which can be considered or understood by itself – a complex organic process implied by each individual stimulus and response involved in it.[74]

The social approach is wide of much that is presently considered central to psychology, but to the extent that the whole pragmatic method Mead and Dewey helped to shape is true, physiological psychology will ultimately have to return whatever data it discovers to the social situation from which all psychical phenomena have arisen. For both Mead and Dewey, Hegel's view of process within a wholeness has not been so much rejected as expanded upon and brought up to date.

IV

EDUCATION · *Philosophy and Psychology in Action*

WHEN the University of Chicago was founded, Chicago was already a center of controversy in education; there were vociferous factions (including the Chicago newspapers) on a variety of questions about the public schools, such as whether the languages of ethnic groups should be taught and whether the curriculum met the needs of particular classes of students. But the most spectacular disagreements gathered around Colonel Francis W. Parker and his Cook County Normal School. Before coming to Chicago in 1883, Parker had made a national reputation as superintendent of schools in Quincy, Massachusetts. There he had stressed individual work with pupils, had given his teachers assistants to help the slow learners, had tried ability grouping, and in general had broken up the routine classroom situation.[1] Parker went from Quincy to Boston for a brief stay as supervisor of primary schools in part of South Boston before moving to the Normal School in Englewood, Illinois. Cook County Normal School, under the Cook County Board of Education and the Board of Commissioners, was composed of classes of student teachers and a demonstration elementary school. Among the educational innovations Parker introduced there were manual training work at the elementary level, activity programs and field trips, the use of a garden in the curriculum, and close cooperation between the school and the parents of the children.[2] The colonel himself was an imposing figure and a powerful orator capable of inspiring strong devotion in his followers. His annual fights with the Board of Education over his budget stirred up county-wide controversy about his educational policies. The colonel always won these battles, one way or another. When the County Board of Commissioners refused to appropriate money for the Normal School and offered the school to the Chicago Board of Education, the fight was moved into Chicago proper. With the help of a number of civic organizations, Jane Addams and Hull House, and Dewey, Tufts, Rollin Salisbury, and Thomas Chamberlin of the university, the school was taken on by the Chicago Board amid loud protests.[3]

But Parker's fights were merely transferred to a new ground, not ended. The same sorts of battles as before took place with the Chicago Board, until at a crucial point, Mrs. Emmons Blaine, daughter of Cyrus McCormick, offered to endow a private school for Parker and his faculty. The Chicago Institute resulted; but Harper very shortly persuaded Parker and Mrs. Blaine to incorporate the school into the University of Chicago, endowment and all. Thus in 1901, the university had a Department of Pedagogy and a Laboratory School under Dewey, a School of Education (as the Institute came to be called) and an elementary school under Parker, the Chicago Manual Training School, and the South Side Academy. Relations between Dewey and Parker had been most amicable up to this point. Dewey later said of Parker[4] that he "more nearly than any other one person was the father of the progressive education movement." * And Parker welcomed Dewey's support as well as Dewey's theoretical statements of what Parker had been practicing for years: "This educational theory I have never been able to state satisfactorily. This is what I have been struggling all my life to put

* At the memorial service held at the university on March 6, 1902, Dewey said of Parker: "Twenty-five years ago, in Quincy, Massachusetts, the work he undertook was an object of derision, as well as of sympathy, all over the country. He was a pioneer, and to many he seemed a faddist, a fanatic. It was only twenty-five years ago; and yet the things for which he then stood are taken today almost as a matter of course, without debate, in all the best schools of this country." *Elementary School Teacher and Course of Study*, 2 (no. 10):707 (June 1902).

into action." [5] But Parker died in 1902, and Dewey became head of the School of Education. The tensions that had begun to build up between the two separate elementary schools came to a head with the merging of the Parker school and the Dewey school. Dewey and the dean of the School of Education, Wilbur S. Jackman, did not get along. Parker had brought Jackman with him to the university, and Jackman was named dean when Dewey was named head of the school. Further, there was dissatisfaction in the faculty about Mrs. Dewey's being named principal of the elementary school; and President Harper notified Dewey in 1904 that Mrs. Dewey's appointment would not be renewed. This last event, among other things, prompted Dewey's resignation from the university.

The point is that questions of education were live ones in Chicago and in the university. Interest in education ran high at all levels in the university in its early days, reaching into almost every department and involving many of its leading scholars. Civic-minded citizens of Chicago were aware that, with rapidly expanding industrialization and a growing immigrant population, the old public school structure was simply not working. It was in this environment that Dewey found support (as well as opposition) for his experiments and a ready audience for his lectures and publications.

Mead was working out much the same ideas as Dewey was on education, but again, Mead published less and more slowly than Dewey, with the result that his work in education was little recognized outside of Chicago. The closeness of Mead's thought to that of Dewey is indicated by the fact, remarked by Dewey in the 1900 edition of *The School and Society*,[6] that Mead and his wife edited Dewey's lectures and saw them through the press. Mead, Tufts, and Moore participated as editors of the *Elementary School Teacher*, and Mead and Tufts were frequent speakers before various education organizations.

In his report on "Three Years of the University Elementary School" in *The School and Society*, Dewey states that he began the school, not with ready-made principles and ideas, but with four problems, the working out of which led to the principles and methods of the school.[7] The problems he lists are these:

1. What can be done, and how can it be done, to bring the school into closer relation with the home and neighborhood life — instead of having the school a place where the child comes solely to learn certain lessons? . . .

2. What can be done in the way of introducing subject-matter in history and science and art, that shall have a positive value and real significance in the child's own life . . .

3. How can instruction in these formal, symbolic branches — the mastering of the ability to read, write, and use figures intelligently — be carried on with everyday experience and occupation as their background and in definite relations to other studies of more inherent content, and be carried on in such a way that the child shall feel their necessity through their connection with subjects which appeal to him on their own account? . . .

4. Individual attention. . . .

Involved in the first problem was the implementation of the social nature of education. The education process itself, within the school, has to be a social affair, an interchange between pupil and teacher and among pupils. But to be educative and not just entertaining or time-consuming, what goes on in the school must be connected with the life and environment of the child outside the school. It was for this reason that Dewey tried to make the University Elementary School an extension of family life, designed to lead the child into other, larger social relations. Parker's idea of the connection between home life and school life became central in the educational theories of Dewey and Mead.* As both pointed out, in the past the child had been an integral part of the getting of food, clothing, and shelter in the family. The things the child did and experienced were integrally connected with adult life about him; even his spontaneous play — hunting, war, cooking — was related to the adult activities into which he would grow. But where the child has no real role in the economy of the family, the connections

* Parker could well have been speaking for the Chicago philosophers when he said: "The ideal school is an ideal community. An ideal community is a democracy, in the purest sense of that pregnant word. Character, constantly realizing itself in citizenship, in community life, in complete living, is the immediate, everlasting, and only purpose of the school." Francis W. Parker, "The Plan and Purpose of the Chicago Institute," *The Course of Study*, 1 (no. 1):10 (July 1900).

between his activities and those of the adult world disappear, and his play becomes a series of disconnected, objectless movements. It falls to the school, then, to take over the former family functions of relating the child to the community in which he lives. The activities to be developed and built upon come from the home and the neighborhood, but the school has the job of connecting them with the interests and movements of the child. In Mead's words, the task of the school is that of "unifying and relating life in the family and the school with stimuli ready to call out the immediate connection between the different spontaneous acts of the child with each other and the life that lies behind them." [8] From the family functions with which the child is already acquainted and in which he has an interest, the teacher can lead him to experiences involving the wider community and natural environment.

The emphasis upon home activities, such as cooking, shopwork, and sewing, in so many experimental elementary schools at the turn of the century was intended to correct the isolation and sterility of the traditional school curriculum. Men such as Parker and Dewey saw most of what went on in elementary schools as the imposition upon the child of an isolated assemblage of miscellaneous facts and skills which might or might not be significant to the child himself outside the artificial situation of the classroom. Education should give the pupil knowledge and not merely what Mead called information: "Whatever is stored up, without immediate need, for some later occasion, for display or to pass examinations is mere information, and has no enduring place in the mind." [9] Most children learn the disembodied data they are expected to assimilate only under the separate motivation of threats of punishment or promises of rewards.

All too often, the only personal relation the pupil has with the teacher is in the imposing of prohibitions. The teacher is disconnected from the data to be learned but is directly involved in the meting out of rewards and punishments. This whole situation promotes learning habits that may prove a permanent detriment to real education. Discipline ought to grow out of the activity itself rather than being externally imposed as it usually is. Here is Mead's statement of the danger:

It is a very real and insistent problem, for our psychology forbids us the use of a discipline that comes back generally to the appeal in one form or another to the comfort or discomfort of the child, his pleasure or pain. A result attained by this means must be very indirect and therefore at great and unnecessary expense. It must set up connections in the child's mind and central nervous system which require a certain amount of violence at first and must be discarded later if he is to use his acquired capacities to good advantage. A child's brain is not an open country within which the pedagogue like the manager of a telegraph company may set up and take down wires at pleasure. A habit that has connected work in school with its comforts and discomforts as motives cannot be dropped at once thereafter to be replaced through the essential relations represented by an interest in the product.[10]

The child can see the purpose in cooking and sewing; the product is immediately useful, and the activity that produces it has a directly perceived relation to the life of the child. He need not be cajoled into such activity or led into it by treating it as a game. And these same activities that connect with the home life of a child can help solve the second problem Dewey listed. An interest in cooking, for instance, can lead to an interest in chemistry, agriculture, industry, geography, history, mathematics, and any number of other areas. This fanning out of interests requires, of course, the intelligent guidance of the teacher. The silly notion, frequently attributed to Dewey in particular and to progressive education in general, that children can be educated by turning them loose in attractive surroundings to pursue their impulses helter-skelter makes no sense in the light of the psychology and social theory of the Chicago philosophers. Experience in any meaningful sense is ordered, and it does not order itself. Our past provides a fund upon which we can draw at any given time, but that fund is available to a child only as he is guided within the social process in which he lives to develop the physical and mental tools or habits necessary to use that fund. The teacher's guidance, moreover, has to be guidance of the *child's* life and interests: "The child who cooks in the kitchen with his mother gets a connection between his playing at keeping house and the reality that is fundamental, but the boy that flaps his arms as wings and hops after imaginary food for imaginary birds is symbolizing essential life processes to his teacher. I doubt if he is to himself." [11]

Dewey deals with the problem of how to introduce subject matters to the child in *The Child and the Curriculum.*[12] There he argues that the child as manifestation of the interests and impulses of its stage of growth and the subject matter as the logical arrangement of a developed body of material are the two end points of the educative process. The former is the point of departure for the teacher and the latter the goal. The teacher has to build upon and direct the interests the child has, in such a way as to enable the child to bring the subject matter in question into his own experience so that the elementary facts of geography or history are significant to him at his own level. Every such expansion of the range of the child's experience by introduction of relevant knowledge becomes, in turn, the base for further expansion in the subject matter in question and in related areas of knowledge. The important thing is that knowledge involves personal experience, as opposed to information as detached items blindly accepted as facts to be learned. Dewey earlier made this clear when he said that "in education we are not concerned with the language that has been spoken, the literature that has been created, the history that has been lived, but with them only as they become a part of what an individual reports, expresses, and lives." [13]

Dewey saw a special problem in teaching children to read, write, and use numbers. These skills are ordinarily taught as abstract disciplines, long before the child is ready for any such abstraction:

Many suppose that abstraction is found only where more or less complex reasoning exists. But as a matter of fact the essence of abstraction is found in compelling attention to rest upon elements which are more or less cut off from direct channels of interest and action. To require a child to turn away from the rich material which is all about him, to which he spontaneously attends, and which is his natural, unconscious food, is to compel the premature use of analytic and abstract powers. It is willfully to deprive the child of that synthetic life, that unconscious union with his environment, which is his birthright and privilege.[14]

The development of the literary skills should grow out of the immediate activities and interests of the student. Dewey goes so far as to suggest that if there is no interest in reading and writing in the first years of elementary school, there will be no great loss if attention to them is postponed until such interest appears. Besides, he says, the very young child is not physiologically ready for the fine adjustment we require of him in reading, writing, and number lessons.[15] And, most important, these essential skills themselves are impaired in the process of their acquisition: "Reading is made an isolated accomplishment. There are no aims in the child's mind which he feels he can serve by reading; there is no mental hunger to be satisfied; there are no conscious problems with reference to which he uses books. The book is a reading-lesson. He learns to read not for the sake of what he reads, but for the mere sake of reading. When the bare process of reading is thus made an end in itself, it is a psychological impossibility for reading to be other than lifeless." [16]

The problem of abstractness is not confined to the three R's or to the first years of school, of course. It can occur with any material and at any level. Mead, for instance, recognized that subjects such as mathematics and physics, because of the remoteness of their concepts from our world of sense perception, manifest the problem of catching the interest of the average student even at the college level. If students have not previously been guided to connect their interests in the world about them to the formal structures of mathematics and science, the college can hardly expect that interest to develop simply upon the presentation of those structures. Mead proposed that the colleges make use of courses in the history of science and surveys of science in order to show the student the connections of scientific discoveries and of scientific methods with other aspects of culture. Social problems are usually evident to the student in a way that scientific problems are not, but if he can be made to see how scientific problems grew out of concrete situations and how the solution to those problems altered the situations, he may lose his sense of estrangement from what he is told the scientist is doing. The techniques and bodies of data of a science may be fascinating to the person already intent upon learning about that particular science, but they are meaningless and dull to many others.[17] Learning, whether of more concrete or more abstract materials, should begin with specific interests and awarenesses of the student, else what is learned is likely to remain detached and without intrinsic significance. At whatever level it is encountered, the problem remains one of making the logical material of the subject matter psychologically relevant to the learner: "Science in the sense in which we can find it stated in books, or set forth in lectures, is not the subject-matter of instruction. Anything that can be found in these forms is simply an index and instrument. It sets before us our goal — the attitude of kind and mind of experience which we wish to induce; when it is read over, into psychological terms, it helps us reach our goal; but without the psychological rendering, it is inert, mechanical, and deadening."[18]

Dewey's fourth problem, that of individual attention, remains one of the most knotty problems of education. With lesson plans and standard tests, the teacher almost has to treat all his pupils the same way — or at least expect the same thing from each of them, even if he recognizes individual differences in the process of attaining the set goals. The system usually sets the goals for everybody. But Dewey saw that any such standardization of what is expected as the result of education must eventuate in mechanization and conformism.

> A truly scientific education can never develop so long as children are treated in the lump, merely as a class. Each child has a strong individuality, and any science must take stock of all the facts in its material. Every pupil must have a chance to show what he truly is, so that the teacher can find out what he needs to make him a complete human being. Only as a teacher becomes acquainted with each one of her pupils can she hope to understand childhood, and it is only as she understands it that she can hope to evolve any scheme of education which shall approach either the scientific or the artistic standard. As long as educators do not know their individual facts they can never know whether their hypotheses are of value.

But how are they to know their material if they impose themselves upon it to such an extent that each portion is made to act just like every other portion? [19]

And, certainly, the kind of psychological awareness on the part of the teacher that the solutions to the previous problems call for cannot be gained except by knowledge of the individual children concerned.

Mass education should not mean that we treat children in the mass. What Dewey, Mead, and many others have been saying for a long time is that if education is worthy of public support, it is worthy of sufficient support to be done properly. Proper education requires enough resources to supply teachers of the kind and number to give children the necessary attention for their development into intelligent, capable human beings. The teacher must have a scientific knowledge of child development that he can apply to a number of children in the different ways called for by the diversity of the children themselves; and that number must be such that a teacher can reasonably be expected to deal with them individually.

The child's individual nature develops in a social setting, of course. And part of his development is in his acceptance of the discipline imposed by that social setting. But just as the discipline from the teacher should arise out of the activity the teacher is guiding, so should the group discipline grow out of the group activities. This socialization of students is, for Dewey and Mead, probably the single most important set of habits the school can inculcate. Because the school presents social situations of manageable size and complexity, it can promote the growth of patterns of activity and of social consciousness that can carry over to the larger, more complex situations of the world outside the school. Working together on projects, children can gain habits of cooperation and a sense of the interdependence of the activities of men. Knowledge and skills can be seen as things to be shared freely for the good of the project in hand, not simply as things to be jealously guarded for fear of giving a rival an advantage in the individual competition that characterizes most school activities.

The sense of shared activity and shared goals becomes less and less frequent as societies become more complicated and industrial processes more technical. The school can become an effective means of overcoming the loss of the sense of community, if the school itself is made a social unit. Habits of social awareness can be acquired in school activities in which students directly perceive the relation of one activity to another and of the activity to their lives. In our world, ends and means become so separated from each other in time and space that any over-all view of social aims as related to the individual's concerns becomes nebulous. Yet, as Dewey says, "A society is a number of people held together because they are working along common lines, in a common spirit, and with reference to common aims. The common needs and aims demand a growing interchange of thought and growing unity of sympathetic feeling." [20] Where a sense of common values is missing, our lives are impoverished. Work becomes drudgery; the various elements of society become opposed factions, in spite of the fact that each is dependent upon the other; and the individual turns to spurious groupings and organizations in the effort to overcome the sense of isolation and incompleteness.

Social awareness is not some additional lesson the school is to attach to its other lessons for the child, however. The point Dewey and Mead make over and over is that learning is essentially social and that social awareness comes naturally when teaching proceeds socially. Learning, as Mead says, should come from the conversation of concrete individuals rather than from pale abstractions of thought. We are social beings; our intellects are social products; and education remains partial and flimsy unless our sociality is explicitly used. Mead calls upon us to see that "however abstract the material is which is presented and however abstracted its ultimate use is from the immediate activities of the child, the situation implied in instruction and in the psychology of that instruction is a social situation; that it is impossible to fully interpret or control the process of instruction without recognizing the child as a self and viewing his conscious processes from the point of view of their relation in his consciousness to his self, among other selves." [21]

The hard thing for many people to see, apparently, is that social development and individual development are not exclusive processes. If the kind of education that imparts a sense of community is done properly, it also will develop and encourage individuality within that community. Too strong an emphasis upon either side of the child's development can lead to misunderstanding of the pragmatists' position. Some of the Chicago sociologists seized upon the social side of Dewey's education theory and proclaimed the primacy of the social in the aims of the school. Ira W. Howerth, for instance, stated his sociological view of education this way: "Society must avail itself of all special aptitudes that will subserve its interests, and must, therefore, raise them to their highest power. The individual aim must not be lost sight of. But the first great demand is progress toward a union of interests. Moral education is of primary importance. The relation of the social and individual aim in education is, therefore, one of superiority and subordination. The primary aim is social." [22] Not all the sociologists concurred in this view, of course. Albion Small, while welcoming the recognition of the social dimension in education, held that the individual still comes first, since "the end of all education is, first, completion of the individual; second, implied in the first, adaptation of the individual to such cooperation with the society in which his lot is cast that he works at his best with the society in perfecting its own type, and consequently in creating conditions favorable to the development of a more perfect type of individual." [23]

Small's statement is closer to the notion of the reciprocity of the social and the individual that Dewey and Mead hold. In Howerth's view, the individual is to be educated for a social purpose and even the development of the individual's own interests is for the sake of society. One of Dewey's central contentions is that education has no purpose beyond itself.[24] Education is not a preparation for some specified or unspecified future but a continuing reconstruction of experience in the light of past experience and present problems. Reconstruction must be made in conformity to social (as well as to natural) realities if individual efficiency is to be increased and satisfactions attained; and the value of the reconstruction must be measured within individual experience with reference to its effect on the social and natural resources available for further experience.

The school has as a primary task the socializing of the child so that he is better prepared for the intricate world into which he must fit than he would be by merely being handed facts and skills in whatever quantity or of whatever sort. Furthermore, on this view, the school is not only a principal means of inculcating social awareness, but an instrument of social change. Not that the teacher has any business indoctrinating pupils with ideas of some new social order. Rather, the pupil, as he grasps the nature of his society and as he is provided with instruments for self-direction in and critical evaluation of that society, will be in a good position to take advantage of the signs of change and to help direct currents of change into desirable channels. The education which merely outfits the student at each stage with the tools for the next higher stage in the educational system may not enable him to cope intelligently with his society; worse, it will probably exclude the student who does not get to the next higher stage from any effective education at all, thereby perpetuating the division between the educated and the uneducated to the detriment of everyone concerned.

Education, at any point, should consist of activities that are immediately meaningful to the student as well as preparatory for further education. Mead and Dewey stressed the need to introduce manual training in the form of handicrafts into the schools to help eradicate the notion of education as learning just for the sake of future learning. The point was not, as it frequently turns out to be, the training of those children who are not expected to get a higher education to enable them to step from school into work at some trade. The point was to guide all children by means of their own activities, bodily and mental, to an understanding of their society and their individual place in it. Students in trade schools, business schools, teachers' colleges, engineering schools are, all too often, cheated of their right to full participation in their cultural heritage. On the other hand, students in preparatory schools, liberal arts colleges, and universities may be cheated of their right to a full sense of the concrete operations that make our society run.

Mead, in particular, saw the practical problem of how to keep the children of the lower economic classes in school long enough to give them some semblance of an education. There was a glaring problem in Chicago in the first part of this century with the great numbers of immigrant workers who poured into that city and its environs. The children of those immigrants (much the same as the Negro and Puerto Rican children in Chicago today) felt alien to the standard curriculum of the schools because of barriers of language, cultural background, economic level, and parental attitudes. As a result, many of these children dropped out of the public schools as soon as possible to take part-time, underpaid jobs and to begin their adult lives too early and too ill-equipped to do any better than their parents had done. Mead saw the introduction of vocational training into the public schools as a concrete step in interesting workers' children and their parents in continuing schooling beyond the bare minimum required by law and as a concrete step to broaden and liberalize the outlook of all the children in the schools about the purpose and operation of industry and science. In an address before the Women's Trade Union League of Chicago in 1908, Mead told the members:

Industrial education means something more than efficiency in shops, something more than technically trained men. It means greater efficiency in the whole community, because if rightly brought in, we are going to have better educated men and women in the community. . . . I have heard an account of a school conducted in Cincinnati in certain steel works there. . . .

These boys to whom I refer were trained of course specifically with reference to work which they were going to do, that of trained mechanics in the shops,—in science, physics, chemistry, and especially mathematics. It would have been possible for this training to have been of a broader character; they could have taken up the history of the industry, the history of the machines they were making use of; there could have been given in connection with this work not only the specific training necessary for their technique, there could also have been given a liberal education; and if the work had been properly given, they would have been just as interested in this liberal education, in this interpretation, as in the mathematics and science essential to the technique.[25]

Mead appealed to labor unions, employers, and the general public on the basis of immediate practical considerations, but he had in mind a much more long-range plan for the schools, as witness the following statement:

> Our great contention is that vocational training be introduced into our school system as an essential part of its education – in no illiberal sense and with no intention of separating out a class of workingmen's children who are to receive trade training at the expense of academic training. We are convinced by what we have found elsewhere in America as well as in other countries that such a division is unnecessary. We are convinced that, just as liberal a training can be given in the vocational school as that given in the present academic school. Indeed, we feel that the vocational training will be more liberal if its full educational possibilities are worked out.[26]

The school that enables the child to relate his learning activities to the larger life around him can function to draw together the various segments of a community and to produce a sounder knowledge of the community on the basis of which genuine progress can be promoted. Mead saw the public schools as possible instruments for overcoming the antagonism between labor and management and for bringing about a richer life for the whole community. Although not as directly involved as Dewey had been in applying his educational ideas in his experimental school, Mead did try in the ways open to him to apply his ideas in the politics-ridden public schools of Chicago. Vocational training was the most readily available and readily acceptable way of introducing into the Chicago schools the kind of social situation that he considered essential for education – the kind of education that socializes the individual and promotes improvement in the society. A different community might find other means more effective; the particular program is not the important thing. Mead simply tried to make use of existing circumstances in Chicago at that time to implement his theory.

The manual arts in the schools are not, for a functional psychology, a training program for mechanics. They are a necessary part of the process of developing the intelligence of the student. Intellect is not a detached mental faculty but a bodily function; and part of the operation of intellect is the coordination of the body, the relation between hand and eye, the ability to shape and manipulate physical materials for some purpose. The advocacy of vocational work in the public schools follows directly from a rejection of mind-body dualism. Education is the guided development of the active functions of the human organism, active functions that are both physical and mental. What Mead was calling for was a program for *all* schools, for *all* children. The segregation of manual training programs, business programs, and college preparatory programs within a school — or even the institution of separate schools for these programs — does not supply the need that Mead and Dewey pointed out. Such segregation is a powerful means of perpetuating economic and cultural class differences.[27]

Because we have for so long relegated the manual arts to an inferior position in our school programs, we find it hard to see any need to include such activity in the already crowded schedules of the more liberal programs. What we expect from the liberal arts programs of the schools is what Dewey calls information, discipline, and culture.[28] The only one of these which the manual training program is supposed to provide is discipline, in addition to certain mechanical skills. The business program is to equip the student with different skills plus a narrow range of information and discipline.

The strictly intellectual side of education is still usually regarded as that part of the school program that imparts information, facts about history, science, literature, politics, the techniques of mathematics, and so forth. The educated man is the informed man; and the greater the mass of information he has, the better educated he must be. And it is easy to test for facts with true-false, multiple-choice, fill-in-the-blanks tests. Tests give us numerical scores to measure information and hence to measure education and intellect. But, as was indicated above by Mead, information is not knowledge. Knowledge requires data, of course, but the data that constitute knowledge are data used, connected with other data and with things, and placed in a context of the life of the knower. In addition to data, however, knowing involves habits of inquiry, of curiosity, of openness of mind, of awareness of the limits of any knowledge. Certainly for the pragmatists, this sense of quest is the vital element in intellectual growth; and no amount of sterile information can replace that sense.

It is at this point that the pragmatists' insistence upon the continuity of the theoretical and the practical has its most important bearing on education. Intelligence becomes a set of habits, not a stock of ideas; an ability to deal with whatever happens to confront you, not a faculty of always giving the expected response; a sense of proportion and of the relative worth of things, not just a knowledge of the acceptable paths. Awareness, capacity, and ways of doing are cultivated by leading the child into scientific inquiry, in the sense that "scientific" is opposed to authoritarian. Such inquiry, as Dewey says, requires at least two conditions: firsthand experience and a problem as the focus of effort.[29] And the intelligence of the child must be respected by giving him more freedom, as his intelligence grows, in interpreting his own experience and in seeking solutions to his problems. Dewey's concept of democracy depends upon just this sort of freeing of the minds of men: "Modern life means democracy, democracy means freeing intelligence for independent effectiveness – the emancipation of mind as an individual organ to do its own work. We naturally associate democracy, to be sure, with freedom of action, but freedom of action without freed capacity of thought behind it is only chaos. If external authority in action is given up, it must be because internal authority of truth, discovered and known to reason, is substituted." [30] Intelligence frees men and makes democracy possible. But the schools impede the growth of intellect so long as they persist in authoritarian methods, however covert. (As when "discussion method" consists in having the students try to guess the answer that the teacher already has.)

Because intellect is not attained in a void, Dewey and Mead maintained that the school should try to direct the activities that the child brings with him from his home and neighborhood to make those activities more meaningful and more effective in the child's life and to enable the child to form habits to help him cope with his world intelligently. It is in this sense that education can exist for its own sake and can be a process that never ceases so long as intelligence continues to function. Formal education should be that special process whereby the immature are equipped to carry on their own education throughout their lives.

The functional conception of education carries with it an answer to the frequently encountered question concerning the obligation of the school in moral training. What is usually meant by moral training is discipline. And discipline ordinarily means obedience, docility, conformity to community standards without question. But if theory and practice are inseparable, then so are intellectual and moral training. The same pedagogical method that makes intellectual training a bitter dose the child has to endure because he is too weak or too clever to resist makes moral training an externally imposed conformity accepted under duress or hope of advantage. The alternative to the legalistic approach to both learning and conduct is sometimes taken to be the approach of making learning and behavior alluring, entertaining. School should be a game and teachers good showmen. Dewey, however, attacked both these methods, which he called respectively the effort and interest theories.[31] He claimed that leading children into activities by sugarcoating them was as damaging morally as coercing children into performing tasks in which they have no interest at all other than avoiding punishment or gaining rewards. In neither case does the child learn to act in terms of the demands of the situation in relation to his own desires and aims. The true ethical function of the school is the development of intelligent, self-reliant, socially oriented individuals capable of acting in their own interests in full awareness of the relations between their individual interests and those of their society.

Tufts addressed himself to the question of moral education in several articles.[32] He argued that in the early school years moral instruction should be left to the indirect agencies of work and cooperation, to the social pressures of the school as an institution, and to the ideals communicated in art, literature, and music. He thought that secondary schools could well supplement these indirect methods by direct study of the relation of the individual to society.[33]

When he came to discuss the ideals to be taught, he cautioned that they must have three characteristics: they must be democratic ideals, they must be moving and not static ideals, and they must be ideals that have a firm hold on reality. And Tufts warned that, while group morality may be democratic, it is not likely to be progressive and that art and literature may be merely visionary and not practical. Therefore he urged as a third agency in teaching ideals the study of life by the scientific method, which in this regard he characterized as recognition of the good there is, how it got here, the basis on which it rests, frank criticism of defects in life, and definite planning to remedy these defects.[34] Presumably, the specific application of the methods of science to moral questions would grow out of the study of social-individual relations that he recommended for high schools. But in all of this, Tufts was just making concrete proposals in line with the functional view of ethics and of education.

One moral question for education of especial moment for the pragmatists is that of competition versus cooperation as the basic relation among men. Tufts looked at both from the standpoint of their results for society. In discussing competition as a social ideal to be considered by the school in moral training, he contends that competition is an agency of progress as it serves to put skills and needs together properly and to bring about new inventions and procedures. Yet, he says, "When competition in business is made to mean, not winning by a better method, but defeating the other man at any cost, it is easy to see that we are ruining the game."[35] And when Tufts discusses elsewhere dominance, competition, and cooperation as types of social organization, he admits that each may contribute to human welfare or, taken abstractly, threaten human values. He claims, however, that cooperation is the greatest of the three and largely the touchstone for the others.[36] Socially beneficial competition, for instance, rests upon a base of cooperation in preservation of the rules and regulations of the activity, whether in athletics or in the business world.

It was in this same vein that Dewey called for the organization of schools on cooperative rather than competitive lines. As distinguished from Tufts's primary concern with the social results, Dewey was concerned with the effects on the individual. In an essentially competitive society, he saw the schools with an opportunity of encouraging a sense of cooperation and social sensitivity that could temper the dog-eat-dog character of much of our economic life. He had no fears that anything the schools would do by way of establishing a cooperative system would crush the competitive spirit of young Americans. On the contrary, he saw that the wrong emphasis on competition in schoolwork effectively kills ambition in some young people at the same time that it overdevelops it in others. He wrote:

Just because all are doing the same work, and are judged (either in recitation or examination with reference to grading and to promotion) not from the standpoint of their personal contribution, but from that of *comparative* success, the feeling of superiority over others is unduly appealed to, while timid children are depressed. Children are judged with reference to their capacity to realize the same external standard. The weaker gradually lose their sense of power, and accept a position of continuous and persistent inferiority. The effect upon both self-respect and respect for work need not be dwelt upon. The strong learn to glory, not in their strength, but in the fact that they are stronger. The child is prematurely launched into the region of individualistic competition, and this in a direction where competition is least applicable, namely in intellectual and artistic matters, whose law is cooperation and participation.[37]

In Mead's language, education is converse, the guided growth of the powers of communication with others and with oneself. And communication is necessarily based on commonality, not on rivalry.

Cooperation is the foundation of society, and morals are social criteria growing out of the relation of the individual to his society. In a 1908 article,[38] Dewey argued that the formal teaching of religion has no place in our schools, because (following Plato) we cannot agree on what we mean by "religion" and because we do not find any teachers of it. He says that religion is too intimate and vital a matter to be taught by external and formal methods. But he had the hope that organizing the school along democratic and scientific lines might bring about a more genuinely religious attitude than our dogmatic, supernatural religions ever produced. Dewey uses Plato throughout this argument; and he refers to Plato's view that any endeavor to teach virtue apart from a reorganization of society and science is sophistry. Dewey uses this view to deny the utility of teaching religion, but it seems to apply (more directly) to the teaching of morals. With the difference, however, that Dewey saw the possibility of democracy and science providing us with a new and better morality, whereas he saw no such result in the case of religion – there he saw only a hope. Dewey and Tufts were both pointing subtly to the impossibility of teaching ethics directly by calling for the use of the social organization of the school and of scientific approaches to knowing in particular as the best means of turning out moral men and women. Not only did the morality have to be implicit in the social situation, but the individual had to see the connection of the action called for to himself. As Dewey put it in an earlier article, "in and so far as the child can not see the meaning and value of his acts and value them for himself, it becomes absurd to insist upon questions of morality in connection with them." [39]

The moral import of school activities depends, again, upon there being a connection between what goes on in the school and what goes on outside it, as well as upon the student seeing some meaning and value in the activity. The school that insists upon enforcing trivial and annoying rules, while basic things go unattended, is working against the formation of moral habits in its students. If morality consists of intelligent habits of action, as the Chicago pragmatists insist, then the proper development of the intellectual powers of the child will at the same time develop good character and the power of judgment. It is when the habits demanded by the school are irrelevant to the purpose of schools and are isolated from the life of the child outside the school that the invidious distinction between the regulations associated with the school and the moral duties of life arises. When the child associates arbitrary authority, coercion, and injustice with the social organization of the school, he is given a poor set of mind for a moral approach to the world at large. This puts a big responsibility upon the schools, and as Dewey often says, we tend to put the whole responsibility there. Education, as one set of institutions among many others, cannot be made wholly responsible for anything. But Dewey, Mead, and Tufts were demanding that the schools be aware of their share in the responsibility for enabling young human beings to discover for themselves some sense of the integrity and value of their selves and of their world.

In much the same way that moral values are implicit in proper modes of action, aesthetic values are incorporated in intelligent activity as appreciation of the fittingness of the various parts of the act with relation to the end sought. The artistic impulses of the child must be guided so as to relate to all his activities. In Mead's words:

> The art impulse in the young child is quite without the impulse to conscious self-expression that characterizes it in the adult. It stands in the midst of the other impulses of the child consciousness with the same value and legitimacy as them all. Like all these its aim is immediate activity. The child draws as he fights or hunts or builds. . . . The pedagogical problem then is of an eminently different nature from that [which] arises with the adult art student, for in its first expression the child's interest lies solely in the immediate activity. The activity is also at first largely isolated. Like all the earlier play-acts the connection with other acts lies underneath and can only be used through such an arrangement of the different activities with reference to each other that the product of the one becomes the stimulus for the next. This is then the thesis which I shall maintain: —The education in artistic expression for the young child involves the recognition of the essential relation between the artistic impulse and the other child impulses and such an emphasis upon this connection that the product of the artistic activity as a stimulus to succeeding acts will rise naturally to consciousness and become a control over the productive act.[40]

Aesthetic and moral values get separated from the process of living because men's activities are disjointed, partial things. Experience does not order itself; one of the main jobs of education is to bring order into the experience of the child so that he sees connections among his random impulses and acts and so that he gets in the habit of seeing connections. Art can be the major factor in conveying a sense of the integrity of life. Just as morality is not just a particular kind of act, so art is not just a particular kind of product. It is an accomplishment in which inner purpose and outer result are felt to coincide. And while this coincidence is fully attained only in those rare instances we call fine art, it accompanies all significant activity and becomes a sign of that significance. As Dewey stated it, in discussing the relation of culture and industry in education:

> Art is not an outer product nor an outer behavior. It is an attitude of spirit, a state of mind—one which demands for its satisfaction and fulfilling a shaping of matter to new and more significant form. To feel the meaning of what one is doing and to rejoice in that meaning, to unite in one concurrent fact the unfolding of the inner life and the ordered development of material conditions—that is art. The external signs—rhythm, symmetry, arrangement of values, what you please—these things *are* signs of art in the degree in which they exhibit the union of inner joyful thought and outward control of nature's forces. Otherwise they are dead and mechanical.[41]

So viewed, art becomes the most complete expression of the order of life, not just the precious product of a special class of people called artists. Art is the contemplative, appreciative element in all action, as morality is the forwarding, expanding element in that action. Educative experience is that experience that enables the person involved to understand and to use the moral and aesthetic elements that experience contains.

A successful institution of this kind of education program would yield men fit for democratic society. Their own powers of mind and will would be developed to deal with the problems of their world; their acts would be done in awareness of the social system within which their acts take place and in awareness of the necessity for a wide variety of contributions to that system and without any sense of class distinction among necessary and useful contributions. Only as a society can produce such men can democracy flourish and can men govern themselves in any effective manner.

For Dewey and Mead and Tufts, their philosophy and their theory of education are meaningless without one another. A philosophy based upon a conception of action must be an active philosophy, and a philosophy acts only by reshaping the attitudes and habits of men. Hence Dewey's assertion that philosophy is the general theory of education.

V

RELIGION · *Philosophy and Psychology in Extension*

PRESIDENT HARPER set the tone for the religious emphasis that characterized the University of Chicago during its early years and for some time after. But, with the exception of Ames, religion was not a central interest of the Chicago philosophers. Tufts did take formal religion seriously, as noted in Chapter I, and he did discuss the church in some of his writings. But he nowhere attempts any systematic treatment of religion. Moore and Mead mention religion only briefly in their work, although Mead left some fragments indicating at least an attempt to come to grips with the problems religion presents. After his pre-Chicago idealistic discussions of religion, Dewey said little on the subject, apart from some statements in the twenties on the renewed science-religion controversy, until 1934 when his *A Common Faith* [1] appeared.* As one of Ames's students, Anna Louise Strong,† said: "The religion of a pragmatist

* Herbert Schneider reports that students at Columbia were constantly asking Dewey to say something about religion. Dewey was finally prevailed upon to read a paper on the subject to the graduate philosophy students, but word got out and people turned up in such numbers that the session was moved to the largest auditorium at Columbia. Dewey was irate. "They just want to see a monkey hang by his tail," he commented; and he said very little about religion at that meeting. He told Schneider that he saw little point in talking about religion, not because he thought it unimportant, but because he considered religion a personal matter.

† Miss Strong remained a disciple of Chicago philosophy only a short time. She made her reputation as a journalist reporting revolutions all over the

is the result of many conditions, one and only one of which is his pragmatism. His pragmatism will undoubtedly determine the form of his belief, but he may not be temperamentally inclined toward the holding of any religious belief at all. The categories of the religious experience may not be vital for his use. My point is this: for a person to whom such categories *are* vital, pragmatism furnishes a completer and more consistently satisfactory response to his needs than absolutism possibly can." [2]

Religious categories were vital for Ames and a number of the students in the Philosophy Department. Ames shared Angell's view that all of philosophy grows out of functional psychology and further maintained that a thorough study of the psychology of religion will eventuate in the recognition and investigation of the basic problems of theology.[3] He and some of his students developed one of the important facets of the wider developments in liberal religion going on in the university and elsewhere. Among others, George Albert Coe of Union Theological Seminary recognized a distinctive Chicago movement centered in Ames's work:

Whoever has observed the recent growth of the functional treatment of psychology must have realized that profound problems are arising for the science of religion. It is true that we are already accustomed to the idea of an empirical, evolutionary, and voluntaristic treatment of the facts of religion. But it is also true that the full purport of this tendency cannot appear until psychology has secured firm control of its own relatively new evolutionary-voluntaristic standpoint. At none of the university centers has the reconstruction of psychological categories in this direction gone on more actively than at Chicago. Here, accordingly, is the radiating center of an active reconstruction of the psychological standpoint with respect to religion. Irving King's dissertation on *The Differentiation of the Religious Consciousness*, which has recently been absorbed into his large and mature work on *The Development of Religion*, Professor Ames's annual course in the university on the psy-

world. The Russians deported her as a spy in 1949, and in the United States she was frequently accused of being a Communist. She has lived in China for some time, and her "Letter from China" was often taken as an officially approved statement of conditions in that country. However, recent reports indicate that Miss Strong, now eighty-three, is out of favor with the Chinese government and may be in prison.

chology of religion, and now his *Psychology of Religious Experience* — these all represent a single movement of reconstruction. . . . The significance of foundation-laying books like this of Ames, therefore, is far greater than ordinary readers will realize. In this work and King's we have the beginnings of an attempt to carry empiricism, voluntarism, evolutionism, and a social view of consciousness to their logical limit with respect to religion. The result is bound to seem revolutionary even to many who are hospitable to all these standpoints.[4]

Irving King's dissertation was published in 1905 and the expanded work in 1910. Coe also mentioned in a footnote the dissertation of Frederick G. Henke, *The Psychology of Ritualism*, published in 1910, the same year Ames's *The Psychology of Religious Experience*[5] appeared.

All these works shared the conception of religion as social in origin, evolutionary in form, and pragmatic in meaning. And there was, in general, a determination to avoid any hint of fixed ontological categories as the bases of religion, as is evidenced in the one objection Ames had to King's 1910 book:

In the treatment of the Mysterious Power, the functional point of view, generally so well employed throughout the book, seems to have been forgotten. Neither the term "concept" nor "impersonal force" is happily chosen in this connection. The savage takes a characteristic attitude in the presence of anything which strikes his attention, anything which is strange, menacing, novel, or surprising. His attitude is that of alertness, caution, and heightened emotion. . . . It is attributing too much to the primitive mind to say that it generalizes these experiences into the "concept" of an "impersonal force" which "resides in" all strange objects. . . . King rightly calls it the "watch-out" attitude and considers it less developed than a notion of spirits. His descriptions and illustrations support this "watch-out" attitude, but to call it Mysterious Power, written with capital letters, makes it seem like a deity of the old, metaphysical sort which has been so erroneously ascribed to the natural races.[6]

Ames is concerned to show that God is a functional concept growing out of the social development of a people, not the result of an intellectual leap attributing supernatural powers to the environment.

Henke wrote an article setting forth what he saw as the main principles of the functional approach to religion,[7] and it constitutes a good, concise formulation of the position. He states the general program and then elucidates five points. His general statement makes clear the distinction of this approach from traditional views:

The functional view of religion represents an attempt to relate religion in all its varied manifestations to the total life-process. It is a direct outgrowth of the point of view employed in biology and functional psychology. Religion is not a something that has been conferred upon mankind, but is itself a type of activity whereby man seeks to adjust himself to his social environment and his social environment to himself. Its *raison d'être* is in the fact that human groups have found and still find it necessary to promote their highest social values. Religion thus becomes an intensely practical affair. It has emerged out of the life-process in the attempt to make life fuller and richer, and finds its place in the life-process because it continues to minister to man's needs.[8]

His five points are as follows:

1. The functional view frees religion from the trammels of legalism and external authority and opens the way for a religion of the spirit. It does this by maintaining that the real function of religion consists in ministering to the ongoing of the highest social process and by insisting that everything that fails to meet this criterion should be expunged.[9]

2. This view of religion is in essential harmony with the view entertained by Jesus. He stood for a complete socialization of the idea of God, and thus brought himself into direct conflict with the *lex talionis* as it was given in Leviticus and Exodus.[10]

3. [The functional view] insists that the test of the highest and most valuable type of religion is not to be found in a past miraculous setting, but in the actual contribution religion makes toward the betterment of human conditions now.[11]

4. The functional view bids a welcome to the evolution of religious thought, practice, and principles. If God has spoken to man in the far past, if he has sought to reveal himself to humanity in olden times, why should he not do so now when man has reached greater intellectual and moral heights?[12]

5. The functional view of religion is a great systematizing and coordinating agency in human experience. . . . The functional criterion of the best and truest religion is, as we have seen, strictly

pragmatic. It asks whether the religion under consideration fits into the rest of human experience, whether it is making a real contribution to the ongoing of the social process. Not dualism of experience, not conflict within experience, but systematic continuous experience is its ideal.[13]

Ames bases his analysis of religious experience on the evolutionary conception: he views religion as arising with social consciousness and representing the most important group interests at a given time.[14] The activities associated with such interests were the bases of the ceremonials and symbols that grew up in the group celebrations of those interests and their objects. He claims, for instance, that nomadic peoples considered sheep as deities, because sheep were the main source of sustenance for the tribe, and that sacrifices were acts of devouring the deity in order to gain some of his magic power. As agriculture developed, cattle became the staple of existence and also the deity replacing sheep. Society became more and more settled and dependent upon outstanding men as rulers and generals, and hence the leaders of the community came to be regarded as gods. It was only a step, as men's interests and knowledge expanded, to a god whose power surpassed that of any man but who was conceived in the form of a man and who shared the interests of men. The scope of the power of these gods was gradually extended beyond the tribe or nation until it was thought of as universal. The might and power of a universal God could have only loose connections with the military fate of a particular group; and as civilization grew, social interests were centered increasingly in problems of justice, so that God became less a warrior and more a judge. In this way, according to Ames, the changes in the concept follow changes in the primary social interests of men; and at any time, different ideas of God grow out of different social situations. In whatever circumstances men exist, they use God to unify their highest values and to make those values more effective in their activities.

The idea of God, when seriously employed, serves to generalize and to idealize all the values one knows. Our actual interests move in the social world and within the vast order of nature. In the simplest reflections upon the facts of life one is led deep into the labyrinth of the natural and of the human worlds. The idea which gathers into itself the interests and values of our daily concerns must therefore signify what are for us the greatest realities in nature and in human experience. To the plain man as he uses the idea of God, in contrast with a passive formal attitude toward it, the idea involves a living process, law or movement, in the working of which human needs are satisfied, justice and truth established, and distant ideals attained.[15]

In the individual also, the growth of religious consciousness is a growth in social consciousness. This, Ames says, is why religious awareness is most pronounced during adolescence.[16] The rise of consciousness of the sexual function increases the adolescent's sensitiveness to other people and to their opinions. Religious education, upon this premise, is nothing more than an intelligent, experimental guidance of the growth of interests of children with special reference to whatever ideal interests accumulate along the way.[17] And Ames agrees with Dewey[18] that adult religious conceptions cannot be imposed upon children in the way adults seem to think this can be done. Religion is possible to the child only as he is able to enter into the social ideals of his community, which, according to Ames, occurs to a very small degree prior to adolescence.[19] He lays down several principles of religious education that follow from a functional psychology of religion: (1) the child is not naturally depraved or in any sense irreligious – rather his activities can be guided so as to become religious or the opposite; (2) the guidance of the growth of religious consciousness should not be attempted by means of imposition of doctrine but through the child's activities, so that his religious nature grows in a way that involves his whole nature, his mind and his emotions; (3) education should recognize whatever psychology discovers about the stages of development through which the child passes; and (4) religious education should be recognized as a continuing process of development, not just a temporary phase ending with the end of adolescence.[20] In the individual, as in society, religion evolves with the evolution of social ideals.

The tying of religion to social ideals imposes a duty upon organized religion to see that its ceremonies and symbols continue to serve those ideals. For instance, most Western religions have built up a complex tradition of rite and language based upon the conception of God as a monarch. We pray for beneficences; we bend the knee before the throne; in many churches we preserve the distinction between the saved and the unsaved, the elect and the damned. Yet, as many liberal theologians have pointed out, we number among our major social ideals that of democracy; not subservience to some higher authority but the right to work with our fellows in whatever ways we can to solve our own problems and realize our own ideals.

A central problem for a functional religion is that of the organization of a church without an authoritative creed yet with meaningful rites that alter with changing knowledge and ideals. What sets Ames apart from the other philosophers as well as from most of the theologians at Chicago is the fact that he was primarily a minister actually applying his religious ideas and testing them in his Hyde Park Church. His church was his laboratory, in a literal sense: "Experiments were being made in education, such as Dewey's Laboratory School in our neighborhood; in social settlements, as at Hull House under Jane Addams; in politics and industry and in the arts. Why not in religion?" [21] Ames tried to make religion meaningful in a world of democratic institutions, scientific advancement, and industrial organization just as Dewey and Tufts tried to do the same thing for philosophy in general.

The experimental church school curriculum he worked out in his church is quite similar in spirit to the curriculum of the early Dewey Laboratory School:

All classes study the vital, recurrent social relations, with material and problems graded to the advancing experience and powers of the children. A wide range of subject matter is suggested to the teachers, according to the interests and capacities of the pupils. So far as possible the particular subjects of study are those that are suggested by the members of the classes from their contacts and work. In a large sense the plan followed might be called the "project method," but the projects are those activities in which all are naturally and constantly engaged, rather than artificially created or imposed activities.[22]

The topics he mentions are those of the home and its affairs, the weekday school and its relations to the home and the community, the city and its government, the state and the nation, the world perspective of Christianity, and the forces of nature. He points out that these are not set topics for a church school but examples of the kinds of topics that were taken from the environment of the children in his church. Exploration of a given subject also involved such activities as seemed appropriate and feasible: programs, dramas, parties, picnics, excursions, and clubs. The main aim was to integrate the church with the lives of its members so that those ideals represented by the church were operative in the lives of the members. In Ames's religion, science provided the intellectual content that constitutes knowledge of the nature of the world, while religion drew together and intensified the attitudes toward and recognition of the valuable possibilities of that world: "Salvation is the conscious participation by thought and deed in this boundless, holy life, rather than the escape from the consequences of original sin and the fall of man. It is won as the soul ripens in knowledge of the sciences, in appreciation of the arts, but above all in faithfulness to the elemental and instinctive relationships of life. Salvation is ethical. It means developed character. It is a life process and signifies the realization of the natural powers of the soul." [23]

Ames succeeded in getting his congregation to accept the Disciples of Christ as the open, progressive, undogmatic sect he saw it to be. It took time and patience, but they even gave up the requirement of immersion for membership in the church.[24] He taught that, as animism and demonology give way to a scientific conception of nature, prayer must cease to be entreaty for magical intervention and become meditation and communion with the spiritual resources of the universe and that religious conversion is, in most cases, a less salutary device for the awakening of religious feelings and ideas than is salvation by education.[25] Ames called for the abandonment of literal dogmas that men who reject magic for science found to be stumbling blocks in the way of their accepting the substance of Christianity. Such passages as the following served to call down on Ames the displeasure of some national leaders of the Disciples sect who were not prepared to abandon all dogmas:

> Miracles and wonders were familiar to the Hebrew mind, as to all primitive minds, and consequently this teacher and leader [Jesus] was accredited with miracles and wonders. It was commonly believed that the gods took the women of the human race for wives, and it was inevitable that as Jesus came to be regarded as a great personage this half divine, half human parentage should be ascribed to him also. That these miracles and this birth should still be regarded by informed men of the present day as actual, literal facts is striking evidence of how much of the primitive age of child wonder and savage credulity still survive in the world.[26]

And, in keeping with his notion of what religion is, he defined churches as "voluntary associations of individuals for the cultivation of the highest forms of life that they can conceive." [27]

There was a marked wariness on Dewey's part in dealing with religion in the early days at Chicago and for some time after. Douglas C. Macintosh,* in a review of *The Influence of Darwin on Philosophy*, took Dewey's reluctance to bring religion into his discussions as a rejection of religion altogether: "It [one of Dewey's fundamental motives] is nothing less than the complete eradication from philosophy of the last vestiges of the positively religious view of the universe. . . . Religion is held to be essentially pre-scientific, that blank submission of the individual, under the compulsion of external authority, to the blank reality beyond, a surrender which was an excusable weakness when tools were rare and clumsy and when, in general, man's command of the methods that control action was precarious and disturbed." [28] Dewey did not allay such doubts when he opposed the teaching of religion in the schools [29] or when he took both liberals and fundamentalists to task for their views on religion.[30]

* Macintosh received his Ph.D. in the Department of Systematic Theology at Chicago in 1909. He arrived at Chicago just after Dewey left for Columbia, but he studied with Tufts and other members of the Philosophy Department. See Macintosh, "Toward a New Untraditional Orthodoxy," *Contemporary American Theology: Theological Autobiographies*, ed. Vergilius Ferm (New York: Round Table Press, 1932), I, 297–300.

When Dewey got around to stating his position on religion, he agreed with Ames on the social origin of religion, but he drew an important distinction between the past social structure of religions and that of the present. Religions were formerly integral parts of the community itself, so that a man was born into a religion just as he was born into a society. But in the modern world, at least in the United States, religion is a set of institutions distinct from the society itself. Society is secular, and most men have to choose a religion rather than being born into one.[31] And while Dewey agrees with Ames that religion grows out of those values man finds in his relation to his environment, Dewey puts more stress upon man's relation to his natural environment than Ames does, although Ames certainly takes both environments into account (see footnote 15 above).

Dewey points out that man is a natural being who achieves whatever ends he does gain by utilizing those natural forces science discloses. Hence all values are results of the union of natural processes and human goals. Religion, then, has as its object the sum of all these unions of man and nature that constitute values.

Dewey's distinction of religion from the religious marks his basic difference from Ames. For Dewey, religion always means *a* religion with its instituted dogmas; religious experience, on the other hand, means any experience characterized by an attitude of reverence for the highest ideals involved in the experience. Ames uses the noun "religion" to indicate those explicit acts of cherishing vital values in ceremonies, symbols, and doctrines.[32] He is concerned with the role of churches as embodiments of religion freed from dogma and outworn symbols and serving as a source of strength and intensity for current social ideals. Dewey objects to the noun and prefers the adjective because "religious," as he says, "denotes nothing in the way of a specifiable entity, either institutional or as a system of beliefs. It does not denote anything to which one can specifically point as one can point to this and that historic religion or existing church. For it does not denote anything that can exist by itself or that can be organized into a particular and distinctive form of existence. It denotes attitudes that may be taken toward every object and every proposed end or ideal."[33] The important thing for Dewey seems to be that the religious is not tied to any intellectual content but that a religion always is. And intellectual assent is a matter for science, not for religion. Ames would agree with this last statement, but he would not deny religion the right to hold doctrines, although he maintains that religion should not be bound by any particular doctrine but should continually seek better beliefs and practices in the light of man's growing knowledge. Ames states this view carefully:

A free church can have no creed. A creed is a statement of belief, "setting forth with authority certain articles which are regarded by the framers as necessary for salvation." . . . If creeds could be regarded as functioning ideologies, summarizing the general attitudes and working beliefs of groups, they would serve a purpose, but they have always tended to become tests of fellowship, rigidly held and often ruthlessly administered. What we do need, and in some form must always have, are general statements of the religious view of life, set in the frame of verified knowledge and of the great objectives of associated human hope and endeavor. Such statements are necessarily subject to change with enlarging horizons and consequent new tasks and problems.[34]

Dewey's turning away from "religion" is a manifestation of his doubt concerning the likelihood of such an institution as the church permitting, let alone encouraging, the openness of mind Ames envisioned. Ames, however, had actually experienced such a scientific spirit working in his own church, and he even saw hopeful signs abroad, such as the growth of community churches.* Dewey does concede that existing churches perhaps can be reconstituted to serve religious ends, but he offers no suggestions for accomplishing this reconstruction. And it is difficult to see how a church can function without converting the religious into some sort of specifiable entity, symbolic or otherwise.

Dewey is willing to use the name God to designate the "*active* relation between ideal and actual."[35] But this relation cannot be

* "Community churches mark a new stage in historic Christianity, a stage in which for the first time the traditional doctrinal standards have been so modified as to be in effect abrogated. The basis of association is practical and empirical." *Religion* (New York: Henry Holt, 1929), p. 278.

hypostatized for Dewey into any kind of thing or system of things, as he makes clear in his exchange with Henry Nelson Wieman following Wieman's review of *A Common Faith*.* This relation is the work of man's imagination and will in unifying his ideals and those natural forces that serve those ideals. Such a conception of God presents additional difficulties for the construction of a church.

Ames conceives God in a more substantive manner. God is idealized reality – order, love, and intelligence – and the idealization of the "practical absolute" in terms of which men have to act in the absence of complete assurance as to the outcome of their acts.[36] And God is personal. Men are part of nature and are persons. Therefore personality is real; and because personality is real and is a value, God includes personality in his being and is personal.[37] Ames compares the personality of God to that of a corporation or other group, his best known comparison being that of God to Alma Mater:

> Alma Mater is not a myth or mere idea. It is the reality of an organization of things and people. Any school boy can appreciate the fact that his college is an entity, objective to himself and yet closely identified with himself and others. Buildings and grounds, endowment money, alumni, donors, faculty, and students belong to it. These are welded together in a life-process, definite and describable. Alma Mater exists in certain forms of activity, in a character which involves specific requirements, offering appreciable rewards for stated conduct and achievement. Toward her, attitudes of devotion and loyalty are awakened. Songs are sung to her, gifts are made in her honor and for her use. Her life flows on through the years, often from father to son, generation after generation.[38]

Ames's God is much more readily symbolized or embodied than a relation is. Dewey asserts the reality of God, but it is the reality of

* "There is a fundamental difference between that to which I said, with some reservations, the *name* God might be applied and Mr. Wieman's attribution to me of something 'that holds the actual and ideal together.' What I said was that the union of ideals with *some* natural forces that generate and sustain them, accomplished in human imagination and to be realized through human choice and action, is that to which the name God might be applied, with of course the understanding that that is just what is meant by the word." "Is John Dewey a Theist?" *Christian Century*, 51 (no. 49): 1551 (December 5, 1934).

any ideal that is effective in action, and Dewey thinks that any attempt to give God a more substantial reality moves us into the realm of the supernatural.[39] Dewey saw benefits deriving from religious movements in the past, but there is little indication that he could see any clear connection between religions as we have inherited them and present problems.

Mead, like Ames, says that "Religion is unquestionably a social affair." [40] And in making his distinction among philosophical disciplines, Mead defines religion in a way close to the definitions of Ames and Dewey: "The religious consciousness is pre-eminently one that recognizes in life a fundamental problem, while it clings to the reality of the great representative objects of conduct which the conflict has abstracted and set before us. In fact, it is allowable to define the religious object as one which, while transcending through its universality the particular situations of life, still is felt to be representative of its meaning and value." [41] The ideals that arise out of conduct may exist merely as ideals in moral thought, but the religious attitude, like the aesthetic, brings into being objects which represent those meanings and values not attained by action yet implicit in our action. Mead represents the religious ideal as being some order of society better than the one in which we live. In traditional Christian thought, this ideal has been that of the Heavenly City or the Kingdom of God. Selves are not "at home" in the world as organisms are, and men conceive a more comfortable world, one in which the conflicts and failures of this one are overcome. Before men had a sense of control over their societies, they could only look to some transcendent power to attain such a world for them.[42]

Religious movements, according to Mead, because they envision a better world, have been instrumental in bringing about social reforms. But with the growth of man's knowledge of his world and the corresponding increase in man's efforts to do something with the world, religion has come to serve a cult value rather than a functional value.[43] And while a cult preserves an ideal, it is essentially opposed to reform of the cult itself, even though the reform is intended to make the cult more effective in realizing the ideal.

The Sunday ceremonial has little carry-over into the weekday world, yet the sacredness of the ceremonial is not to be questioned. The tendency of religion to become a cult gives Mead at least an analogous problem to that Dewey has with respect to the function of churches.

Despite this difficulty, Mead recognizes religion as one of the possible universalizing forces in society; economic activity is the other. Religion utilizes the universal concept of brotherhood; economics the concept of exchange.[44] But as religion takes on the qualities of a cult, the attitude of identification with mankind is induced only in the Sunday ceremonials and remains isolated from most of our activities. Thus religion loses its effectiveness as a universalizing force and, Mead says, cooperative endeavor with other men in some kind of team work becomes a more useful and perhaps a higher form of identification with others.

In two unpublished fragments,[45] Mead throws some additional light upon the problem he finds in organized religion.* In the first, he discusses the forms religious emotion may take. Like any other emotion, it can be cultivated for its own sake, with the usual abortive effects for action:

> As long as the emotional element serves only as the means of subjective evaluation and reinforcement of the act, it will be controlled by the activity itself and the life process within which it lies. E.g. in animals, since the sexual emotion together with the whole process, is but a function of reproduction, it, as well as the process, is under the control of this periodic activity. But when the aim of activity is to bring about simply the conditions that are requisite for an emotional paroxysm all control is lost. The only limitation that is set to such indulgence, is found in the exhaustion of the organism in its effort to produce these arbitrary situations. But this exhaustion does not mean the passing on to the next appropriate phase of the life-activity, for the emotional element has been taken out of its setting and remains a never ceasing demand upon the organism. . . . Undoubtedly there is a great deal of religious emotion that is of this type[.] [W]e are wont to term it sentimentality when we recognize it as such, and while it may not have as

* The fact that they were not published is of some significance in evaluating Mead's views on religion.

disastrous effects as some other types of dissipation[,] we find the same tendency to deform conduct. What should be the spring to healthful action becomes only a means for arousing feeling. Perhaps no better definition can be given of religious cant than the ideas, phrases and formulae into which everything is forced to produce certain religious emotions.[46]

But religious emotion may also function positively with relation to action:

In three ways then the appeal to emotions apart from the acts to which they belong may be of organic value—in keeping before consciousness ideas which cannot pass into action, in stimulating certain valuable activities which have through ritual a symbolic meaning[,] and finally in assisting to abstract from hemming and confining environment and so giving opportunity to other activities to come to expression.[47]

Mead distinguishes the negative and positive functions of emotions as "the difference between self-indulgence and the use of the emotions for the sake of subjective freedom—what is commonly called inspiration." In every positive case, action follows upon the emotion. "Action is the result and normally in such instances the whole phenomenon turns upon the decision to take an important step. This step[,] however[,] is not the form in which the problem presents itself. The question is not in a typical case of conversion whether one will give up certain habits and adopt certain other courses of conduct—but whether one will conform to a certain religious attitude which carries with it these actual changes and innovations in conduct." [48]

In every case, the emotion gives significance to the action of the individual, according to Mead. The first positive form of religious emotion gives a meaning to the individual's activities with reference to some social situation beyond the one in which he finds himself. This social ideal cannot be acted upon directly in present circumstances, but it can make otherwise apparently futile forms of behavior reasonable and rewarding, because of the ideal kept in the agent's mind by its emotional power.

Again, when new activities are beginning to emerge but are not yet consciously apprehended, these activities may be promoted by the emotional effects of ritual observances.

It is when we are unable to get the bearings and full meaning for ourselves of a new line of conduct that we appeal to an emotional expression, which lies beyond our present selves, for freedom from the immediate environment and for the inspiration to go on to something larger we are not able to state and which we accept therefore in a certain sense on faith. This is a very curious and to my mind a very subtle phenomenon and one which no ethical writer has fully analysed. . . . The phenomenon stated in its simplest terms is the appearance in consciousness of new phases of conduct whose value is represented not in intellectual but emotional terms. That new lines of conduct should appear is not strange nor that they should come to appeal to us for their value to ourselves and to society, but that this appeal should come in such tremendous power to the emotions before men are in any position to estimate their value intellectually is certainly strange. E.g. How shall we explain psychologically the emotional outburst of the time of the Reformation. Actually there was ushered in at that period the principle of individual control of action on the basis of immediate social consciousness, in the place of authority. Undoubtedly the possibility of such an advance was to be found in industrial and commercial condition[s] in which the individual found himself in control and was forced to depend upon his own judgment. But the generalization of these facts into a political formula did not take place for centuries yet. . . . In the place of such positive intellectual formulae we find the powerful religious movement which demands[,] however[,] of those who shall pass under its power the assumption of a certain definite outward attitude toward the representative of authority in its most universal terms—the Romish Church. Along with this goes the restraint from the amusements and especially social entertainments which represent satisfaction with and acceptance of the existing conditions. The general attitude is that of clearing the ground for a new type of activity which has not yet appeared—at least not definitely in consciousness. It seems to me psychologically impossible to explain this situation unless we assume that the emotion really represented an activity that was developing instead of one already present.[49]

Finally, religious emotion may serve by abstracting from existing conditions to free new and vital sources of energy.

In England, the emotional outburst that affected the whole nation from the top to the bottom, and was represented not only by the Methodist revivals but also by Shelley[,] the Lake poets and later by Chartism and Carlyle, was made psychologically possible by a subjective abstraction from the existing institutional and social conditions; and the continued existence of such states of consciousness resulted in an attitude that was peculiarly favorable to the political activity of classes of society which had been without representation before. Much the same may be said of the religious revivals that are identified [with] the name of Jonathan Edwards, opening the way for the larger politics of the revolution, while those aroused by the preaching of Finney and Lyman Beecher stand for the awakening that preceeded the active politics of the anti-slavery movement. To put this statement in a different form[,] the intellectual attitude of the idealist is favorable to radical action and the abstraction from the immediate environment and its customary value for the individual, which characterises the outburst of religious or allied emotions, gives us practically the intellectual attitude of the idealist.[50]

All these positive functions of religious emotion are coincident with certain kinds of social forces and their positive quality continues only so long as they continue to operate in conjunction with those forces. But still the problem remains of how to institutionalize religious emotion without divorcing it from the conditions of society that give rise to it.

In the second paper, Mead examines the Christian principle of love from the standpoint of the psychology of emotion. He distinguishes the gospel of John the Baptist from that of Jesus: John could only preach repentance of sin and performance of the duties of life, whereas Jesus preached love of God and man as "the fulfilment of the entire law and the source of the right will." Love here is the expression of the sense of the identity of interest of all men, of the universal community of man. This identity of interest is the basic relation of the Kingdom of Heaven, in which all men are brothers. The Kingdom is a qualitative condition, not quantitative, as is illustrated by the parable of the workers in the vineyard. Once accepted into the brotherhood, there is no distinction between those who have been laboring long and those who have just begun.

According to Mead, the emotion of love that betokens the spirit of brotherhood is the source of the energy and will that give rise to the actions of brotherhood. As he concludes,

if the principle which Jesus represents is to be expressed as an emotion, the emotion of love, it can only be as an action principle – the principle of the most complete and absolute activity our natures are capable of. It must have back of it the instinctive actions of the whole social[,] in other words religious[,] nature[,] and it must have the power of supporting these activities at once and without cessation. To sit back and enjoy this emotion must be more unallowable than in the case of any other because it should [be] the supreme emotion of life[,] that is the emotion that calls for the most unceasing and most supreme action of which we are capable.[51]

Mead's treatment of Jesus' relation to the Jewish religion he sprang from is enlightening. In it, he compares Jesus' role to that of Socrates:

There is then a real analogy between Socrates and Jesus. Socrates represented the Greek intellect upon which Greek religion[,] Greek traditional morality necessarily went to pieces, and the Greek traditional state instinctively turned upon him and administered the cup of hemlock. Jesus represented the right will which loved God with all the heart and one's neighbor as oneself – which as the fulfilment of the entire law necessarily resolved into dead letters the ritualistic service upon which the Jewish nationality was formed. And the Jewish state turned instinctively upon Jesus and crucified him.[52]

The Jewish religion was a cult and Jesus changed it into an active principle. Our problem is that of how to keep the principles set forth by Jesus active. As Mead said elsewhere, if an ideal can be acted upon, to confine it to a cult is to sterilize it and eventually to kill it.

A cult is an instituted social habit, and so long as it evokes its emotions with reference to situations that are not actual – such as the brotherhood of man – so as to play some positive role in the situation that is actual, the cult is socially valuable and a universalizing force. But, unfortunately, a cult holds on to its imaginary objects in a fixed fashion no matter what changes take place in the actual world. In this way, cult value comes to be opposed to functional value. Mead uses the church as the prime example of the cult function in its isolated preservation of the idea of a social order that does not exist. Economic institutions stand at the other end of the scale as purely functional. As Mead says, "The economic man may be an abstraction, but he certainly exists and functions, and we need no cult to keep alive the faith in the functioning of money, though there is hardly an agency that has had more profound effects in bringing all men into association with each other." [53] The end of the exchange process is necessarily a functional one; that of religion can easily be detached from the activities of life because of its remoteness from life. Business is palpably real; the brotherhood of man remains only an ideal.

Yet Mead acknowledges that religion is potentially the more profound force for bringing men together, even though economics has been more effective.

> Exchange is the life-blood of the economic process, and that process abstracts everything from the other individual except what is involved in trading. The religious attitude, on the contrary, takes you into the immediate inner attitude of the other individual; you are identifying yourself with him in so far as you are assisting him, helping him, saving his soul, aiding him in this world or the world to come – your attitude is that of salvation of the individual. That attitude is far more profound in the identification of the individual with others. The economic process is more superficial and therefore is one which perhaps can travel more rapidly and make possible an easier communication. The two processes, however, are always universal in their character, and so far as they get expression they tend to build up in some sense a common community which is as universal as the attitudes themselves.[54]

And Mead is talking about religion in an institutional sense, just as he is talking about economics in an institutional sense. Ends, desires, and attitudes are effective in the world only as they are given body in social organization. The two universalizing institutions fall at opposite poles of cult and function, with all other institutions falling somewhere in between. The problem of religion, for Mead, then, is that of how to make the church more functional and less of a cult.

Tufts's view of religion seems more orthodox than that of any of the other Chicago philosophers:

> The religious has always implied some relation of man's life to unseen powers or to the cosmos. The relation may be the social relation of kin or friend or companion, the political of subject to a sovereign, the cosmic relation of dependence, or that of seeking in the divine completer meaning or more perfect fulfillment for what is fragmentary and imperfect. In its aspect of "faith" it holds all these ideals of power, wisdom, goodness, justice, to be real and effective. The moral, on the other hand, concerns itself, not with unseen beings or cosmic reality, but with human purposes and the relations of a man to his fellows. For religion, conscience may be the "voice of God"; for morality, it must be stated in terms of thought and feeling. The "moral law" must be viewed as a law which is capable of being approved, at least—and this implies that it may also be criticized—by the mind. . . . Instead of regarding its standards as laws established once for all by a divine authority, morality seeks to reach *principles*. Instead of embodying its ideals in persons, the moral seeks to reshape them continually. It is for religion to hold that "God reigns," and therefore "All's right with the world." The moral as such must be continually overcoming evil, continually working out ideals into conduct, and changing the natural order into a more rational and social order.[55]

At the same time, Tufts did not see the problem Mead saw in connecting religion and action: "But when once a distinctively moral function or social relationship has been incorporated into the conception of the deity,—when the god is protector, judge, father, husband, or redeemer of kin, all the added sacredness of religious conceptions is transferred to the moral. Wrong becomes sin; iniquity becomes impurity; the awfulness of Sinai invests the moral law; the mystic vision, the emotional seizure, become the initial impulse to a life of moral enthusiasm and spiritual power."[56] Perhaps it is this orthodoxy that enabled Tufts to observe traditional religious rites without raising the embarrassing questions that bothered his colleagues.

Tufts certainly recognized the necessity for change in our religious ideas along with changes in the world. For him, this meant at least two things: the continuing reinterpretation of the great religious teachings and revelations of the past and the application of our religious ideals to the central activities of our lives. Among other things, the first requirement means that religion must be given a social significance, rather than just an individual one, in the light of our knowledge of the social nature of man.[57] And the second means that the preacher must shift his admonitions from the language of kinship and politics to that of economics and science, because the major problems men confront today are not in the realm of father-son or sovereign-subject relations but in that of relations of exchange and inquiry.[58] The religious problem for Tufts, then, was that of readjustment within the church and its doctrine in the face of changing knowledge and conditions, not that of the viability of the church itself.

Unlike James, Dewey did not see as a primary task of pragmatism the rescue of religion from the onslaughts made in the name of science. Where James was alarmed by the attacks on religion by extremists such as William K. Clifford, Dewey was concerned with bringing the methods of science into philosophy and as a result emphasized the positive rather than the negative aspects of the growth of science. The churches stood as bastions of conservatism in a world Dewey saw as one of increasing possibilities for human betterment. Because of this outlook, Dewey had less faith in the probabilities of reconstructing religion by reconstruction of the churches than Ames and Tufts did. Dewey agreed with Ames that the religious attitude should permeate a man's whole life, but Ames saw the church as promoting this integration of values while Dewey saw the opposite: "The attempt to segregate the implicit public interest and social value of all institutions and social arrangements in a particular organization is a fatal diversion."[59] For Ames, the church is to serve to focus attention on and arouse interest in the integration of man's highest social values in such a way as to connect that attention and interest to all the activities of life. For Dewey, this very focusing carried the danger of fixing those ideals and of separating them from the functional activities of men. It was just this fixing and separating of ideals that Mead saw as characteristic of a cult.

But Dewey's reservations about churches as organized religions is a reflection of his general reluctance to deal very explicitly with any ideals of wide generality. He preferred to leave implicit any overarching ideals involved in his philosophy, out of fear of anything that smacked in any way of an absolute. So it is easy to see why the notion of a church deliberately organizing men's highest ideals into a concrete institution would be anathema to him.

Mead shared Dewey's distrust of churches, yet Mead realized the positive function of religion and understood that that function was necessarily a social one and thus had to be instituted in some way. The very fact that religion promoted emotions attached to nonexistent communities gave religion its importance as a social force when those emotions were kept functional with relation to actual communities. Mead also knew that such emotional attachment to goals reaching far beyond what is could not long survive without embodiment in symbols and ceremonials. And there must be some organization of persons and things to serve as trustee for those symbols and ceremonials. The fact that religious ideals are no longer incorporated into the fabric of the community as a whole but are found in a special institution within the larger institution of the community presents the difficulties both Dewey and Mead saw. And whereas Dewey made clear in his writings on ethics that the individual and the social sides are inseparable and tried to maintain the two sides in balance, his religion is weighted on the side of the personal and individual, in spite of its social content. In the light of Dewey's philosophy in general, it is difficult to see how he thought that the values represented by the religious attitude could be developed or perpetuated apart from some sort of institutional embodiment. Mead saw the problem in better perspective, perhaps, but he did not undertake the task of trying to work the problem out in the light of his social psychology.

So, of the Chicago pragmatists, Ames is the most pragmatic, the most empirical of the lot in his view of religion. Tufts seems to take the church for granted as the bearer of religious values. Dewey almost loses sight of the empirical requirements for religious ideals to be effective. Mead keeps those requirements in mind, but in a purely theoretical way. Tufts and Mead tested their ideas about society by getting into the thick of social action in settlement work, labor disputes, and educational matters. Dewey did the same thing, particularly in his early experiments in education and his later involvement in social and political movements. But only Ames really tested his ideas in the realm of religion.

Ames's attempt to make sense of the reality of God in terms of a philosophy in which reality is determined by experience is to compare the personality of God with that of a corporation or college community, operating through individuals but having an existence distinct from any given set of individuals. God is real in a structure or order of things and men directed toward the realization of the social good. Ames tried to establish in his church just such a realization of the religious ideal of love and brotherhood. The realization was, of course, incomplete; but the partial objectification of such religious ideals in the institution of the church was for Ames fully analogous to other institutional realizations of ideals. Dewey's Laboratory School was far from the ideal educational institution Dewey had in mind, but it was considerably closer to that ideal than were most of the schools he saw around him. Ames regarded his Hyde Park Church in almost precisely the same way. Schools have changed in the United States in response to experiments like that of Dewey's school and to his ideas. Churches have also changed because men like Ames tried to put new religious ideas into practice. Ames had, it must be added, rather highly favorable conditions for his experiment in Hyde Park. His was not entirely a university church, but he drew largely from university people for the leadership of his congregation. Therefore he had a more enlightened, more open-minded congregation than the average pastor could expect, and so he could introduce innovations with some expectation of getting the cooperation of those involved. The same thing was true of Dewey's school. He, too, drew upon the university community for support—and for pupils. If he had not been able to count upon a considerable amount of tolerance and open-mindedness on the part of the parents of the children in his care, his schemes could not have gone far. And, with respect to the effects of the two experiments, it is doubtful whether Dewey would see schools of today as any closer to the educational ideal than churches of today are to Ames's religious ideal. Dewey's ideas on religion reflect the fact that he did not try to put them into practice as he did his ideas on education and that he did not see them in the world around him as he did his ideas on ethics and politics.

There were many men outside the Philosophy Department in the University of Chicago who were working in religion, of course. The Chicago School of Theology grew up largely in the Divinity School and made its mark as a front-runner in espousing the liberal religious views that flourished in the first quarter of this century and that have continued to influence religious thought in America. Shailer Mathews came to the university in 1894 and established ties with Albion W. Small and the Sociology Department in developing his social gospel. George Burman Foster was at Chicago from 1895 until 1918. His views were initially derived from those of the German liberal theologians Albrecht Ritschl and Friedrich Schleiermacher, and his first reactions to pragmatism were negative.[60] But Tufts points out the change Foster underwent from his initial rejection of pragmatism and functionalism: "His [Foster's] philosophical basis he found, not in the idealism which had earlier held sway in Germany and was, when he began to work, predominant in British and American thinking. Nor did he adopt as a whole the method and point of view of the pragmatic movement although he regarded the conception of evolution as crucial in his problem, and says in his preface to the second edition of the *Finality* [*The Finality of the Christian Religion* (Chicago: University of Chicago Press, 1909)] that this movement presented a new situation which would compel a rewriting of his manuscript for the projected second volume."[61] And Tufts's judgment is borne out by the account Foster takes of functionalism and pragmatism in *Christianity in Its Modern Expression*,[62] even though he is still critical of them at various points. Gerald Birney Smith reflected much the same influence Foster did and was at least working in the same general way Ames and others were, as Shailer Mathews indicates in a tribute to Smith: "I am repeatedly reminded of his clear insistence on the significance of method as a substitute for external authority. . . . he illustrated a new theological method – the concentration of effort upon religious and moral experience rather than upon doctrine." [63]

Other men important in the liberal theology movement at Chicago were Ernest DeWitt Burton, Shirley Jackson Case, Henry Nelson Wieman, and Bernard Eugene Meland. Among the eminent theologians produced by the University of Chicago are Winfred Ernest Garrison, Douglas Clyde Macintosh, Clyde Weber Votaw, and William Kelley Wright.

Apart from Wieman's avowed debt to Dewey and to Mead,[64] it is difficult to say exactly what influence the functional psychology and pragmatism of Chicago had on its theologians. The empirical approach to religion had started elsewhere and was being widely practiced. But Chicago was a center of development in religion just as it was in other fields. The excitement of the intellectual atmosphere made ideas contagious and openness to what others were doing almost a necessity:

A university full grown at two years old! Nothing like that had ever happened before. The spirit of adventure and discovery was in the air. It was like being among the Argonauts, the comrades of Drake and Magellan, and the 'Forty-niners, all at once. Yet the place was rich in the heritage of ancient and modern cultures as well as in the zest of academic pioneering. Seeds of new learning were being sown with lavish hand for future harvests, but meanwhile whole groves and forests of the full grown trees of erudition had been transplanted for immediate fruit and shade. There was such a thrill of new adventure as two-hundred-year-old Yale had not enjoyed since the days of Elihu himself; and at the same time there were ripe scholars from England and Scotland and Germany and from the older American seats of learning, about whom nothing was new except their association in this place and the fresh enthusiasm which the novel scene and the incomparable Harper aroused in them.[65]

Whatever the impact of Ames and the other philosophers on the theological developments at Chicago, their work was a major factor in the general movement to free religion from dogma and authority.

VI

SOCIOLOGY, ECONOMICS, AND POLITICAL SCIENCE · *Applied Pragmatism*

THE Chicago philosophers were directly involved in psychology, education, and religion. The reach of their ideas was not confined to those areas, of course. But there is more difficulty in establishing the influence of ideas where the connections are not so direct. The empirical approach in general and the pragmatic approach in particular were part of the intellectual climate in the first quarter of this century. Otherwise it would be impossible to explain the pervasiveness of those approaches in so many areas at Chicago as well as elsewhere. And while there were certain key figures in the spread of the new empiricism, there was a genuine interchange of ideas going on in the university, so that the term "cross-fertilization," which was frequently used to refer to the situation there, is more apt than the term "influence."

At least two additional fields were affected by the pragmatists in a direct enough way that they deserve specific notice, however, and a third was sufficiently in the pragmatic tradition to be mentioned. Mead was the long-standing mentor of many of the sociology students at Chicago, and as will be indicated below, some of them felt that they were closer in spirit and letter to Mead's philosophy than any of the later philosophers were. Dewey helped give a new direction to the economic thought of some of the major economists of the period, both through his classes at Chicago and through his continuing philosophic presence there after he went to Columbia. And Charles E. Merriam, the major figure in political science at Chicago, was at least in the new empirical wave with the philosophers and others.

Albion Small built the Department of Sociology into a center of social studies that dominated American sociology during much of this century. Of the first forty presidents of the American Sociological Society, sixteen of them were Chicago Ph.D.'s and four others were on the Chicago staff. In the same period, the Chicago department produced more Ph.D.'s in sociology and placed more of them in colleges and universities than did any other university.[1]

Small and Dewey jointly published two of their essays, Small's "The Demands of Sociology and Pedagogy" and Dewey's "My Pedagogic Creed." [2] And Small and Vincent's *An Introduction to the Study of Society* [3] had earlier reflected much the same empirical concern that his colleagues in philosophy were committed to.* The sort of orientation toward practice that distinguished pragmatism marked Small's thought and caused him to insist all his life upon the centrality of ethical principles for sociology: "From the human standpoint no science is an end in itself. The proximate end of all science is organization into action. The ultimate interest of the sociologists, therefore, is in turning knowledge of the social process into more intelligent promotion of the process." [4] And Small's reputation seems at this point to rest largely upon his practical accomplishments: his department, the *American Journal of Sociology*, and the American Sociological Society. Much of his writing is concerned with establishing the province and the importance of sociology as an intellectual discipline, but his success was greater in the realm of practice than in that of theory.

Charles Richmond Henderson came to Chicago with Small in 1892 as assistant professor of sociology. Like Small, he arrived at Chicago two years before Angell, Dewey, and Mead and had already formulated his basic position. But also like Small, he found

* "In the present stage of social thought, it is much more important that students of society shall acquire a right habit of inquiry than that they should learn any one's conclusions about social relations" (p. 31).

functional psychology and pragmatic philosophy provided reinforcement for tendencies he already had. The tone of Henderson's *The Social Spirit in America*[5] was that of a pious Chautauquan, talking about a mystic world wisdom guiding man's destiny. Yet, in the same book, he calls for human activity as the only basis for achievement. And his essay "Practical Sociology in the Service of Social Ethics"[6] takes a strong stand for relating science and practice. Here he calls for attention to the practice of theory, points out the need for scientific norms, and sees practical sociology as a guide to experiments in social method. He supports his arguments by reference to work done by Dewey, Mead, and Small. Henderson early moved into the Divinity School and was head of the Sociology Department there until his death in 1915.

George E. Vincent, who was co-author of *An Introduction to the Study of Society* with Small, received his Ph.D. in 1896. Ira Woods Howerth received his in 1898. Both men were primarily concerned with sociology in its relation to education during their tenure in the Chicago department. Vincent left Chicago in 1911 to become president of the University of Minnesota and later president of the Rockefeller Foundation. Howerth went to Colorado State Teachers College in 1921 as head of the Department of Sociology and Economics.

While the connection between Small and the Philosophy Department (especially Dewey) is apparent, that between the philosophers and some of the men who got their degrees in sociology at Chicago is even clearer. William Isaac Thomas, whose work on the Polish peasant is a milestone in American sociology, studied under Dewey and Mead, and his early book, *Source Book for Social Origins*, makes use of some of the basic conceptions of functional psychology:

Control is the end to be secured and attention is the means of securing it. They are the objective and subjective sides of the same process. Attention is the mental attitude which takes note of the outside world and manipulates it; it is the organ of accommodation. But attention does not operate alone; it is associated with habit on the one hand and with crisis on the other. When the habits are running smoothly the attention is relaxed; it is not at work. But when something happens to disturb the run of habit the attention is called into play and devises a new mode of behavior which will meet the crisis. That is, the attention establishes new and adequate habits, or it is its function to do so.[7]

This view is obviously based upon the conception of the role of problems in thought and action set forth by Dewey and Mead. The ideas that the subjective side of experience arises from some interruption in an ongoing activity (habit) and that action is the movement to restore the activity are fundamental to the Chicago pragmatism.* Thomas went on to develop sociological principles different from those of attention, habit, and crisis, but his general methodological approach continued to be a functional one. Ernest W. Burgess, a student and later a colleague of Thomas, called attention to this source of Thomas's thought: "In his general orientation he was profoundly affected by the pragmatic philosophy of John Dewey, whose influence still pervaded the university although he had departed for Columbia five years earlier, by the social thinking of George H. Mead, also a colleague, and by the anthropological studies of Franz Boas." [8]

Robert Ezra Park came to the Department of Sociology in 1914 largely through the efforts of Thomas. He had been a student at the University of Michigan, where he got to know Dewey and Mead. Park is best known for his pioneer work in human ecology and more especially for his study of the city. He and Burgess acknowledge their indebtedness to Thomas's *Source Book* for the point of view and scheme of organization of their *Introduction to the Science of Sociology*.[9] Park is in the empirical tradition of the pragmatists, but his specialized studies show less direct carry-over of explicit philosophical and psychological concepts than Thomas's work does.

One of the closest ties between sociology and philosophy at Chicago was that established by Ellsworth Faris. Faris received the

* See the discussion of these topics in Chapters II and III above in connection with Dewey's articles on the theory of emotion and on the reflex arc concept, and Mead's articles on the psychical and on the philosophical disciplines.

Ph.D. in psychology at Chicago in 1914. He was an avowed follower of Mead, and his major lifelong interest was in social psychology. When Faris took over as head of the Sociology Department in 1925, Small was an old man and the department had dwindled from its stellar days to a point where only Small, Ernest W. Burgess, and Faris remained. Faris brought Park back to Chicago and added William F. Ogburn, Samuel Stouffer, Louis Wirth, and Herbert Blumer in sociology, and in anthropology he brought in Ralph Linton, Edward Sapir, Fay-Cooper Cole, and Robert Redfield. Faris tells that Mead asked him to give an introductory course in social psychology that Mead's own course could presuppose. The closeness of the relation between Mead and sociology is further indicated in Faris's account:

All advanced students in sociology were sent into Mead's course; and it is worth recording that, when Mead was stricken in the early part of his last quarter of teaching, the philosophy department approached us to find someone to carry on the course, a task which Professor Blumer of the department of sociology performed to the satisfaction of us all. At present the course on social psychology does not appear in the offerings of the philosophy department, and in the University of Chicago it is the sociologists who are trying to carry on the tradition of Mead.[10]

Not only did Faris feel that it was the sociologists who were the continuers of Mead's thought, but he also considered the volume some of Mead's students in the Philosophy Department had compiled to present Mead's social psychology as something less than an accurate account. In a review of that volume, *Mind, Self and Society*, Faris said:

But Mead never wrote his book on social psychology. The present volume was assembled from the notebooks of students who heard him in the latter part of his career. The editor has, unfortunately, seen fit to give it another title and has taken the liberty to rearrange the material in a fashion that will be deprecated by many who knew Mead and thought they understood him. . . . Mind, self, and society is the reverse order to that which the structure of Mead's thought would seem to make appropriate. Not mind and then society; but society first and then minds arising within that society – such would probably have been the preference of him who spoke these words. For societies exist in which neither minds nor selves are found, and it is only in human societies that a subject is its own object — only in these is there consciousness of self. Man, he held, is not born human; the biological accident becomes a personality through social experience.[11]

There was a standard comment around the Philosophy Department for a long time after Mead's death that Charles Morris, the editor referred to, had been expected to "assume the mantle of Mead." But Morris had decided instead to don other garb.

Faris did not write his book on social psychology either. He did publish a volume of his essays, however, in which he was the stout defender of Mead's views. And he sketches, from his vantage point, the roles the members of the Philosophy Department played in advancing social thought:

> This discussion has been concerned with the direction in which current scholarship has been trending. The part played in this development by the members of the Department of Philosophy at the University of Chicago has been entirely worthy of the traditions of our group. Professor Tufts has emphasized throughout his teaching career the social influences in the development of personality. The chapters which he wrote in the Dewey and Tufts *Ethics* not only revealed a thorough mastery of sociological and economic writings, but served to define for the younger men of that day the problem of the relation of the mores to the moral life of the individual.
>
> In the lectures and writings of Professor Moore the stress has been placed (at least this was true when the writer was a student) on the analysis of the thought process, and later students of social psychology have derived much inspiration and received much clarification from his formulation of instrumentalism. The relation of conflict to reasoning makes essential the discussion of association with others and leads inevitably to a repudiation of the older atomistic individualism. Indeed, the accusation of solipsism which was heard in the early days of the pragmatic controversy was utterly unfounded, chiefly for the reason that individual mind is essentially social in its constitution.
>
> Professor Ames repeatedly acknowledged his obligation to the social point of view and made a notable contribution in his *Psychology of Religious Experience*. The analysis set forth of the essentially social character of the individual's religious experience added a strong tower to the structure of the temple. When religion

is defined as the consciousness of the highest social values there is made possible a method of study of religious experience through social psychology which was previously not available.

In the case of the present writer, the greatest obligation is felt to Professor Mead, to whom American scholars are indebted for some invaluable and wholly unique contributions. Nowhere can be found a comparable analysis of the psychology of meaning, the nature of symbolism, and the distinction between the significant symbol which makes human experience possible and the inferior development which accounts for the limitations of the lower animals. Mead's doctrine of the histrionic designated as the tendency to "take the role of the other," has, in the opinion of the writer, been one of the major contributions in this generation to our knowledge of how the personality develops and the consciousness of self arises. Mead has set forth the process by means of which the spontaneous and meaningless gesture is defined by the responses of the other, so that, while our ideas are our own and the symbol is private, yet the soul of the symbol is its meaning, and meaning is the contribution of others.[12]

Burgess, Wirth, Blumer, and Redfield had all done their graduate work at Chicago and were intimately acquainted with Mead's thought. But, while the early theoretical concerns of men such as Small and Thomas reflected rather clearly the same kind of ideas Dewey and Mead were teaching, the later more specialized concerns of the sociologists showed the influence of pragmatism and functionalism only indirectly in their methods and attitudes.

Charles A. Ellwood studied under E. A. Ross at Cornell as an undergraduate, and in Berlin in 1897 he worked with Gustav Schmoller, Georg Simmel, and Friedrich Paulsen. But his graduate work at Chicago in 1896 and again in 1898–99 was to provide him with the basic form within which his conception of sociology was to develop. Ellwood became chairman of the Department of Sociology at the University of Missouri in 1900, and he made that department a major force in the growth of the discipline of sociology. He counted among his students such sociologists as E. B. Reuter, Herbert Blumer, C. C. Zimmerman, and Luther L. Bernard.

From the time he wrote his doctoral thesis, published as *Some Prolegomena to Social Psychology*,[13] Ellwood argued against the attempt to interpret society in purely objective terms. He insisted that such an attempt to reduce sociology to a physical science is an impossibility in view of the essential part values must play in accounting for social action. He follows functional psychology (as opposed to its extreme behavioristic offspring) in finding it necessary to retain "subjective" terms such as feeling, intelligence, value, even while he insists also that "objective" concepts such as activity, habit, adaptation, stimulus, response, are to be utilized as far as they are adequate to the purposes of the sociologists: "As regards 'objectivism,' while the author holds to the objective method in the broad sense of the term and believes that objective terms should always be preferred to subjective terms in social description, when it is possible to employ the former without ambiguity or loss of clearness, yet he also holds that a radical objectivism in the social sciences is, from the nature of the phenomena with which they deal, impossible. . . ."[14] To support this view, he offers the considerations that society is essentially an inter-subjective relation, that civilized man lives in an ideational rather than a perceptual world, and that centrally initiated psycho-neural processes are vital for the social life of man.

In line with this method for sociology, Ellwood held out against those who would make social science "value-free":

> . . . it is impossible to study those collective processes without perceiving the immanent values. It is impossible, for example, to study social organization without perceiving social maladjustments or possible economies not realized. It is impossible to study social changes without seeing advantageous and disadvantageous adjustments. It is impossible also to study the various types of social organization without indicating the superiority and inferiority of the various types, or to formulate a theory of social progress without implications of social obligation. . . . Knowledge of values grows directly out of knowledge of facts, and all generally accepted valuations . . . are collective processes having reference to the totality of life conditions. It is impossible to have knowledge of facts without judgments of value becoming more or less attached to those facts. In other words, judgments of value inevitably mediate between action, on the one hand, and pure or theoretical knowledge, on the other.[15]

Although in his later book *The Psychology of Human Society* he claims that this is an entirely new work restating the theories of his earlier books from a more objective and scientific point of view, he still emphasizes the importance of subjective data and still lists as fundamental sociological concepts most of the same concepts he had been using all along: social process, coordination or coadaptation, cooperation, conflict, and the like.[16] Most of these terms and their use Ellwood derived from Dewey and Mead. In fact, he says in his thesis and elsewhere that he is just extending to society ideas about the individual he got from Dewey's advanced psychology course.[17] And in his book on religion, he relies often on Ames's statements of the religious interpretation of pragmatism.[18] But while he remained tied, at least to some extent, to the approach and terminology he got at Chicago, Ellwood did not always satisfy his former teachers with his statement of that position, as Tufts's review of *Sociology in Its Psychological Aspects* indicates:

> . . . although the author sometimes speaks of the intellect as instrumental for adaptation to environment — as though the environment were "here" already and man's only task were to fit into it — the prevailing thought is rather of creating by ideals a "subjective environment" toward which the objective environment is to be shaped. This is not to make intellect instrumental to a (non-intellectual) life-process. It is rather to bend the life-process toward standards and ideals which could have no existence without intellect. Intellect, does not merely "function" by "mediating" social adaptations; it is itself a creative agent, a constituent factor in determining what the adaptation shall be. I do not mention this ambiguity because it is peculiar to Professor Ellwood's discussion. It is not infrequent, but the two interpretations mark fundamentally different views as to consciousness.[19]

Yet, however orthodox or the contrary he may have been in teaching and publishing a functional theory of sociology, Ellwood has to be classified as an influential product of the Chicago School, through both his writings and his students.

In less overt and openly acknowledged ways, many of the leading sociologists of this century also carried the pragmatic conception into their discipline all over the country. Edward Carey Hayes,

Luther L. Bernard, Emory S. Bogardus, Edwin H. Sutherland, Edward B. Reuter, Walter Bodenhafer, Howard Jensen, Roderick McKenzie, Dwight Sanderson, Frederick Detweiler, and Everett C. Hughes are only some of the American sociologists who are Ph.D.'s from Chicago. And Kimball Young studied with the Chicago philosophers before getting his Ph.D. in psychology at the University of California. It is an almost impossible task to try to assess the degree to which these various sociologists were shaped by the ideas of Mead, Dewey, and others. Most books on the history and development of sociology give a prominent place to both Dewey and Mead and credit them with a strong influence upon most of the Chicago sociologists. A typical report is this one from Maurice R. Stein: "One seminal theorist in this tradition [which Stein calls dramaturgic] was George Herbert Mead, whose *Mind, Self and Society* nourished an entire generation of social psychologists. Mead was a colleague of Park and clearly influenced Park's conception of social psychological processes at many points. Everett Hughes has come closest to achieving a synthesis of Mead's study of symbolic processes with Park's interest in urban patterns." [20] Of course, what the social psychologists were nourished on were the lectures upon which *Mind, Self and Society* was based, and Faris at least implies that the two may not be identical. And such statements of clear influence are easier to state than to establish.

There is no doubt, however, that Mead in particular had an enormous impact upon sociology both directly upon his students and indirectly through them. Mead and Dewey together (in the early days at Chicago physically together and later together in spirit) probably did as much to shape American social science as any two men can be said to have shaped such a sprawling and diverse set of disciplines.

When we turn from sociology to the other social sciences at Chicago, the identifying of connections with the philosophers becomes even more difficult. There was no explicit link in a course or personality, in the sense that Mead, and later Faris, provided a live liaison between philosophy and sociology. There were students, of course, who crossed departmental lines regularly and deliberately and took ideas and attitudes with them from one place in the curriculum to another. Certainly this was true in the field of economics.

J. Laurence Laughlin, who came to Chicago in 1892, was a staunch defender of orthodox economics, as evidenced by his textbook which consisted of Mill's political economy with the social philosophy left out and Laughlin's comments added. But Laughlin's orthodoxy, which no doubt stood him in good stead with Harper and Chicago's trustees, did not prevent his recognition of the intellectual power of Thorstein Veblen, who proved in the long run to be the most radical of the attackers of economic orthodoxy. Laughlin had taken Veblen under his wing at Cornell, and he brought Veblen with him when he came to Chicago. Not as a member of his faculty, however, but as a fellow. Veblen rose very slowly through the ranks of reader, instructor, and finally assistant professor in the period from 1892 to 1906. During this period, he published his *The Theory of the Leisure Class* [21] and *The Theory of Business Enterprise*,[22] as well as important articles which later appeared in *The Place of Science in Modern Civilisation* [23] and *Essays in Our Changing Order*.[24]

Veblen had received a Ph.D. in philosophy at Yale in 1884 with a dissertation on Kant. Even so, he went to Chicago as a student in 1892. During his stay at Chicago (and Veblen outstayed Dewey by two years) he and Dewey were very much aware of each other. Some commentaries on Veblen attribute his general scientific outlook to Dewey, as well as his biological-psychological approach to economics. And Dewey credits Veblen with teaching him the distinction between business and industry. But with two such original minds, it seems pointless to try to trace the origin of ideas they shared. Each took whatever ideas he found fruitful and made them his own in his distinctive way. Veblen put it well when after the death of Robert F. Hoxie, a former student of Veblen's, he was asked how much influence he had had on Hoxie. He replied that it was about the same as Hoxie's influence on him.[25] Something of the same relation held between Veblen and Loeb. Veblen found Loeb's concept of tropism a useful one; and Loeb, in turn, made use of Veblen's instinct of workmanship. Veblen may have been a student in rank when he arrived at Chicago, but he was not a student in mind. He was thirty-five years old and was already developing the original ideas that were to cause such a stir in the academic world.

There are obvious parallels between the philosophy Dewey was working out and the social analysis Veblen undertook. Veblen's insistence that economists must turn from deducing systems from unquestioned and frequently unrecognized preconceptions to the observation of the economic activities of men was a manifestation of the same concern that motivated the whole empirical movement. And his awareness of the poverty of the hedonistic psychology upon which he saw orthodox economics based led him to demand a more adequate psychology which is more closely related to biology, whereas some of his fellow economists (including Herbert J. Davenport, another of Veblen's students) were claiming that economics could just ignore hedonism and psychology altogether. Veblen's reliance upon the orientation, at least, of functional psychology has led Paul T. Homan to assert that "In his efforts to bring a realistic psychology to bear upon the problems of human activity, Dewey was forging instruments for Veblen's hand." [26] Veblen was not a man to accept ready-forged instruments from anyone, however. In his own evasive style, he would seem to be setting down precisely the tenets of functional psychology:

According to this view, human activity, and economic activity among the rest, is not apprehended as something incidental to the process of saturating given desires. The activity is itself the substantial fact of the process, and the desires under whose guidance the action takes place are circumstances of temperament which determine the specific direction in which the activity will unfold itself. . . . The economic life history of the individual is a cumulative process of adaptation of means to ends that cumulatively change as the process goes on, both the agent and his environment being at any point the outcome of the last process.[27]

But instead of avowedly accepting any such tenets, he proceeds to say that they may be better or worse than earlier views, the point at issue being simply that they are in line with current scientific thinking and that therefore the social sciences must follow the drift since they cannot avoid being caught in it. What Veblen is doing, of course, is to state in a most oblique way that the new psychology is the latest and most adequate set of hypotheses; but that he, in true scientific fashion, refuses to stamp that set as true or to commit himself to more than a tentative acceptance of it. Psychology and physiology must each pursue its own end; Veblen's end was not theirs. But he did use their findings and those of other disciplines insofar as he found them fruitful in his own pursuit of knowledge.

Veblen had been aware of Dewey's philosophy (and Mead's) since their days at the University of Michigan. He makes almost no reference to the Chicago philosophy, however. It is not until 1923 that he refers to Dewey, in his *Absentee Ownership*.[28] Meanwhile he took quite a few jabs at pragmatism in his earlier writings. It is not always clear just whom he intends to include under the term "pragmatism," and he thoroughly confuses the issue in the midst of one of his attacks on "pragmatism" by a favorable reference to James's discussion of the making of theories in his *Psychology*. And in another place, Veblen takes the trouble to point out that he is using "pragmatism" in a more restricted sense than that commonly used by the pragmatic psychologists. Where they extend the etymological sense of the term to include any action with purpose as well as action in which knowledge is to serve some expedient end, he uses it only in the latter sense. But despite these disclaimers, he does seem to set forth a conception alien to functional psychology and its accompanying pragmatism in his idea of idle curiosity. For, whereas James, Dewey, Mead, and other pragmatists account for "disinterested inquiry" as arising out of problematic situations, Veblen contends that idle curiosity is the result of a distinct organic development in response to inhibitive nervous complication. One reaction to this complication is a motor impulse directed to some expedient outcome for the organism; the other, he says, does not spend itself in motor conduct and is not directed to use. As a matter of fact, he says, "Pragmatically speaking, this outlying chain of response is unintended and irrelevant."[29] And this same sharp distinction recurs in his discussion of the difference between the professional and technological schools and the pursuits of scholars and scientists.[30]

This difference with the pragmatists (James and Dewey, not Peirce) did not affect what Veblen did when he was inquiring into social and economic processes: he was investigating economic activity; it only made a difference in what he saw as his reason for that investigation. But it is difficult to read Veblen's incisive, acid prose as "purely scientific inquiry." It all sounds like the voice of a man intensely concerned with the practical world of industry, business, and education. At the beginning of his attack on pragmatism, Veblen admits that his objections to the new philosophy do not mitigate the usefulness of it for his investigations:

> In dealing with pedagogical problems and the theory of education, current psychology is nearly at one in saying that all learning is of a "pragmatic" character; that knowledge is inchoate action inchoately directed to an end; that all knowledge is "functional"; that is of the nature of use. This, of course, is only a corollary under the main postulate of the latter-day psychologists, whose catchword is that The Idea is essentially active. There is no need of quarreling with this "pragmatic" school of psychologists. Their aphorism may not contain the whole truth, perhaps, but at least it goes nearer to the heart of the epistemological problem than any earlier formulation. It may confidently be said to do so because, for one thing, its argument meets the requirements of modern science.[31]

Hence the fact remains that Veblen wrote in the same spirit as functional psychology and pragmatic philosophy. He could not but have been reinforced in his convictions about this approach to economic problems by the success of that approach he saw all around him at Chicago. The philosophers, sociologists, and others there were, in turn, reinforced by him in their certainty that theirs was a more promising mode of inquiry than were past modes. Veblen cannot justly be said to be an outgrowth of the Chicago philosophy, but he can certainly be said to have been a senior partner in the expansion and application of it. The closest Veblen ever came to acknowledging this relation probably was the reply Dorfman reports a somewhat mellowed Veblen to have made after hearing an attack on Dewey and James by a latter-day behaviorist: "He will never know as much as Dewey and James forgot." [32]

Not all the Chicago economists shared even the cautious use Veblen made of functional and behavioral psychology and pragmatism. The attack Veblen (and others later) made upon the hedonistic preconceptions of orthodox economics appeared to Herbert J. Davenport as a move into the province of psychology, a move he considered not only needless but dangerous for an economist. As was noted above, in the face of the disagreements Davenport saw in psychology, he maintained that economics could and should ignore the whole controversy. All that the economist requires, according to him, is the twofold assumption that man has desires and makes choices. Beyond that assumption, the economist cannot wait for the psychologists to settle their quarrels nor can the economist enter into them. If the economist tries to do the former, there can be no hope for any development of his discipline for a very long time to come; if he tries to do the latter, he simply confuses his discipline with problems he is not competent to solve.

If only the philosophers and psychologists could agree! And so long as they can not or will not, what is there for the economist safely to do? For my own part, I am content to agree with both — in the sense that I prefer a view which dodges these puzzling and complicated issues, committing myself to neither. . . . For myself it seems sufficient for immediate purposes — and safe withal, since all the warring schools so far agree — to hold merely that men do desire and do choose. I find it unwise to accept hedonism, but unnecessary to reject it. I am content to forego certain attractive fields of analysis until the scouting squads of these other sciences have made them safe for untechnical wayfarers — the thickets cleared, and all ambushing patrols accounted for. [33]

And earlier in the same article, Davenport asks that the economist bow out of the arena of controversy over value. Here again, the economist should distinguish the particular kind of value he is concerned with and leave any other considerations to those disciplines fitted to deal with them:

. . . But if value is to mean to the economist merely relations of exchangeability, it should mean solely and always this one thing, connoting always the idea of rate or ratio; or, if this be overmuch to ask of frail human thought, the term *price* should be substituted for *value* wherever the objective facts of the relations of goods in the market are to be expressed. This would mean the abandonment of the term *value* to the uses of the other sciences to make whatever best they should be able out of its various vaguenesses.[34]

Although Davenport got his Ph.D. at Chicago in 1898, he had published two textbooks in economics before he arrived there. And while he later was regarded by some of his fellow economists as a radical, he undertook to revise certain economic doctrines in terms of what he saw as actual economic conditions, but to revise them within the general framework of orthodox economic theory. Like Laughlin's, however, Davenport's orthodoxy did not prevent his admiration for Veblen; and it was to Davenport that Veblen owed his job at Missouri.

Wesley Clair Mitchell, who received his Ph.D. the year after Davenport did, failed to see any of the pitfalls Davenport saw in the expansion of the scope of interests of the economist. Mitchell embraced the pragmatic outlook of Dewey and the biological bent of the new psychology, as well as the sociological orientation of Veblen. From Veblen, Mitchell learned to look afresh at the problems of economics, to question the psychological assumptions of economic theory, and to view economics as a human concern broader and more vital than the dismal science inherited from the nineteenth century. Mitchell appreciated Veblen as a pioneer, but he viewed Veblen as a speculative thinker whereas Mitchell saw the requirement in economics for empirical inquiry on the new base rather than for further speculation. And Dewey gave him the general methodological base from which he proceeded to his own empirical, quantitative studies of business cycles and other phenomena of the economic organization he found functioning in the United States. Mitchell's economic studies were not philosophical exercises in the realm of economics but detailed statistical analyses of specific economic institutions. He found in the Chicago philosophy a framework within which he could locate and direct his economic work: "Human nature is in large measure a social product, and among the social activities that shape it the most fundamental is the particular set of activities with which economists deal."[35] While the new psychology gave him a conception of behavior and of society, his professional concern was with that "particular set of activities with which economists deal."

Mitchell's own account makes explicit his debt to Dewey:

> . . . John Dewey was giving courses under all sorts of titles and every one of them dealt with the same problem—how we think. I was fascinated by his view of the place which logic holds in human behavior. It explained the economic theorists. The thing to do was to find out how to attack certain problems; why they took certain premises as a matter of course; why they did not consider all the permutations and variants of those problems which were logically possible; why their contemporaries thought their conclusions were significant. And, if one wanted to try his own hand at constructive theorizing, Dewey's notion pointed the way. It is a misconception to suppose that consumers guide their course by ratiocination—they don't except under stress. There is no way of deducing from certain principles what they will do, just because their behavior is not itself rational. One has to find out what they do. That is a matter of observation, which the economic theorists had taken all too lightly.
>
> A brief introduction to English economic history by A. C. Miller, and unsystematic readings in anthropology instigated by Veblen reinforced the impressions I was getting from other sources. Everything Dewey was saying about how we think, and when we think, made these fresh materials significant.[36]

In a true pragmatic fashion, Mitchell was applying the principles of pragmatism in order to find out about economic functions in the society by use of the best instruments he found at hand or could shape for himself. He did not ignore psychology as Davenport tried to do; nor did he backhandedly acknowledge it as the best there happened to be at the time. Mitchell admitted that functional and behavioral psychology gave him a fruitful orientation toward the problems he undertook to solve; they did not serve to impose anything upon his solutions. Mitchell's solutions were elicited from the data he could get and were justified by their relevance as explanations of concrete economic processes. He thereby served to verify the ideas of the pragmatists in a most admirable way—admirable because he tested their principles in an area other than that from which the principles were induced. Thus, once again, the intellectual debt was a mutual one.

In the case of Robert F. Hoxie, we have no such indications of the impact of what was going on in philosophy and psychology at Chicago while he was a graduate student there. He received his Ph.D. in 1905; therefore he was in the presence of the same activities Mitchell found so stimulating. Mitchell, however, took a minor in philosophy while he was majoring in economics; Hoxie did not. Hoxie's major work was in the field of labor economics, and his problem method in economics, together with the terminology he used in his analysis (such as functional types of labor union), has led historians of economics to classify him as a pragmatist. But Hoxie himself gives no such account as that of Mitchell, and he does not refer to his philosophic colleagues, as Mitchell does, with the exception of one reference to Mead on the development of labor unions in Hoxie's book *Trade Unionism in the United States*.[37]

Pragmatism in economics is clearly and avowedly represented, however, in the work of Clarence Edwin Ayres, who along with Veblen and Mitchell is usually classed as an institutional economist. Ayres took his degree in philosophy rather than in economics, writing his dissertation on the relations of ethics and economics. From Tufts he learned the essential interconnection between social and individual development:

> Assuming the notion, of which he had been an early exponent, that mind is something which is developed in the course of societal evolution, he has gone further and described moral evolution as a process in which the moral faculty is sharpened by a growing social order, while at the same time the social structure is built up by the exercise of a developing moral consciousness. But the most significant feature of Professor Tufts's statement of the nature of the development of morality is his full recognition that the gradual moralization of society through the evolution of social conventions is but one aspect of a process which includes as its other phase the development of the moral character of the individuals who compose society.[38]

But Ayres says that his most profound obligation is to Dewey, even though Dewey had long since left Chicago when Ayres arrived. The pragmatism that he found congenial led him directly to Dewey, whose social interests were closer to the concerns of Ayres than were the historical interests of Tufts or the social psychology of Mead or the logical interests of Moore. The second most important source of Ayres's approach to economics was Veblen, who likewise was gone from Chicago by the time Ayres got there.

Ayres's initial analysis of economic phenomena was an application of the basic structure of the pragmatic analysis of the act to the history of economic theories.[39] He argued that a social crisis calls forth criticism of existing institutions and of the economic theories that fail to deal with them. As a result a new theoretical structure is erected to deal with the crisis, but in order to have the new theory accepted the economist must make it logically airtight, must argue that it is founded on ultimate reality. Such a theory is then preserved for its own sake as a truth; schools develop; left and right wings crop up. But meanwhile new crises are arising, and the systematic theory proves inadequate to them. *Ad hoc* solutions are proposed, until the body of economics outside the theoretical orthodoxy becomes more important than the orthodoxy itself. This external theory is then systematized to fit the particular problems that called it up, and the whole procedure begins all over again.

Ayres offers as evidence for this thesis the history of economic theory from Adam Smith to the beginning of the twentieth century. Smith, according to this interpretation, set forth his principles merely as means for the solution of the immediate difficulties he saw in his society. His successors proceeded to turn his principles into a system, at the same time that they lost sight of his problems. As a consequence, these systematic principles served less and less to make clear the nature of the new problems that arose with the passage of time and the growth of industrialism. The neoclassicists tried to patch the system up to meet the new needs, but the time finally came when the system began to appear superfluous for the actual dealing with economic processes.[40]

Thus Ayres pointed the way for economics to become an evolutionary science in the sense in which Veblen had seen that it was not. Economics could be a body of theory being developed consciously in response to changing economic processes and problems. And in whatever sense Veblen disagreed with the pragmatists about the distinction between theory and practice, Ayres at any rate was solidly on the side of the pragmatists:

However "pure" a science may be, however remote from "practical affairs" may be its search for the ultimate, it must proceed from the conviction that ultimate truth is somehow worth having, that having it would somehow make a difference in men's lives. The difference between sciences in point of practicality, therefore, seems to be, not even a difference of degree – since the most absolute science must contribute to some human need – but rather a difference in the nature of the problems of living to the solution of which the sciences contribute. The essential thing for every scientist to understand is, therefore, not whether his science is "pure" or not, but what the actual problems are about which all his scientific studies must be massed.[41]

His critical view of our society, a view in which the central role of technology as source of the implements of change is basic, is set forth as the result of the application of Dewey's theories to the problems of economic institutions. And time has not altered Ayres's adherence to what he perceives as the spirit of Dewey's philosophy. In his *The Theory of Economic Progress* in 1944, he said:

The application of Dewey's theory of valuation to an understanding of the meaning of value in the field of economics, toward which the present discussion is attempting to move, goes beyond Dewey's published works. But surely it is implicit in his essay on the "Theory of Valuation" (1939) . . . And equally surely the application is bound to be made, in a world in which the published works of Dewey and Veblen, for example, coexist and are bound to be read occasionally by the same people.[42]

He reiterated this program in *The Divine Right of Capital* in 1946:

The way of thinking of which he [Dewey] is the most eminent exemplar has a host of practitioners scattered through a wide variety of intellectual disciplines and fields of inquiry. If it has affected economics less than many other fields of study, that is largely because of the natural persistence of eighteenth-century philosophy in a discipline which was an offshoot of eighteenth-century philosophy; and if the present writer is an exception to this rule, he is by no means the only one, and the fact is no particular credit to him, since he grew up in the atmosphere of instrumentalism.[43]

In his essay "Veblen's Theory of Instincts Reconsidered," [44] Ayres again paid his respects to Dewey as the intellectual messiah of the twentieth century.

A few words perhaps should be said about Henry W. Stuart in connection with the economics that was affected by pragmatism. As was pointed out in Chapter I, Stuart was one of the early graduate students in the Philosophy Department, receiving his Ph.D. in philosophy in 1900. But before he got his degree, he had joined forces with Veblen in the attack upon the psychological bases of classical economics in a pair of articles that appeared in the *Journal of Political Economy* in 1895 and 1896.[45] His essay "Valuation as a Logical Process" in *Studies in Logical Theory* continued his criticism of marginal utility, as did the later essay, "The Phases of the Economic Interest," in *Creative Intelligence*. Stuart's work was much used by all the early institutionalists, but he turned from economics to philosophy, where he developed a moral theory that eventually veered considerably away from his youthful pragmatism to a Kantian position.

As was noted in Chapter II, Stuart conceived ethics and economics as exhausting the field of value. The ethical judgment has to do with conflict of ends, wherein a harmony is sought between an old pattern and a new purpose; economic judgments, on the other hand, deal with apportionment of limited means between ends which, as such, are not incompatible. Aesthetic experience, for him, is post-judgmental; hence it has no logical function and cannot be called value. This truncated view of the act of reflection leaves out the part played by man's feeling nature except as emotional energy constituting a purpose. The feeling enters only after the fact as immediate appreciation of an attained adjustment between the agent and his world.[46] Stuart's failure to accept the basic pragmatic concept of the interrelations of feeling, thought, and action as grounded in the problematic situation was an early indicator of the impermanence of his pragmatism.

Veblen, Mitchell, and Ayres were hybrid products of philosophy and economics, as Thomas, Ellwood, and Faris were of philosophy and sociology. In political science, Charles E. Merriam was less a hybrid than an alert and open observer of what was happening in philosophy, economics, sociology, and other disciplines.

Harry Pratt Judson, the first head of the Department of Political Science, was initially hired by Harper in 1892 as professor of history, with principal duties as Harper's assistant in organizing the university. Judson's career was mainly administrative: he became dean of faculties, dean of graduate studies, and, upon Harper's death, president of the university. It remained for Merriam to create a productive political science program on a par with those in the other social sciences.

Merriam came to Chicago from the pioneer Political Science Department at Columbia. His education and early writings were in the historical tradition of the discipline, and the stance that has won him a place among the founders of scientific political thought took form after he went to Chicago in 1900. His program evolved gradually, and the department's most creative period began in the 1920's. The book that established Merriam as one of the significant moving forces in the attempt to make politics a science, *New Aspects of Politics*,[47] was published in 1925. That book became a bible for many of the younger men in the field, and is still regarded by many as a landmark.[48] The Social Science Research Council, for which Merriam is usually given credit, was established in 1923.

The stream of distinguished Ph.D.'s in political science that came out of Chicago began in the twenties, too. Although the output began later than that in some of the other departments, it is fully as impressive, and includes Leonard D. White (1921), Harold F. Gosnell (1922), Harold D. Lasswell (1926), Frederick L. Schuman (1927), Valdimer O. Key, Jr. (1934), C. Herman Pritchett (1937), David B. Truman (1939), Avery Leiserson (1941), Herbert A. Simon (1943), and Alfred De Grazia (1948). Since most of these men came after the most active period of the Philosophy Department, their work shows fewer signs of the philosophy than that of the sociologists or economists.

Merriam was in communication with the philosophers and others at Chicago, of course. In writing of his early years there, he said: "Here the shape of Charles E. Merriam was modified by his contacts with the sardonic Veblen, with friendly John Dewey, with helpful Tufts, and with associates such as Wesley C. Mitchell and H. J. Davenport, intent on economic conquests." [49] And the plan he set forth for political science in *New Aspects of Politics* was clearly in the spirit of his colleagues at Chicago. He called for the application of the methods of science to social and political phenomena, deliberately pushed aside any suggestion of specific types of political organization in the interest of emphasis on conscious direction of evolving political forms, declared for politics as the science of intelligent social control, and sought an end to wrangling among political theorists in favor of cooperative inquiry.

But Merriam was intent upon separating himself from his early theoretical and historical researches and separating political science from history and philosophy. He recognized the pragmatists' efforts to relate philosophy to the social world, but he emphasized the decline of philosophic speculation in political science in the twentieth century. Not that he repudiated the role of political philosophy: he simply chose not to enter that field in order to devote his energies to encouraging empirical research by means of polls, surveys, election studies, and the like. Philosophy was one of a number of disciplines political science could utilize in its own special inquiries, along with history, sociology, economics, statistics, psychology, biology, engineering, anthropology, and ethnology.[50] The political scientists were part of the interchange that characterized Chicago,[51] but Merriam indicates the nature of his relation to philosophy in his remark that "For many American students interest in general philosophy has been implicit rather than explicit." [52]

The "school" that Merriam headed was really too diverse to fit that title, as Heinz Eulau points out.[53] Merriam encouraged a wide range of approaches and interests among his students, and the characteristic they had in common was energy in attacking all sorts of political problems. Lasswell, for example, brought the techniques he had acquired from psychology, psychiatry, and psychoanalysis to bear on political behavior. Gosnell and Key explored methods of voting analysis. Schuman's interests were in international relations, White's and Simon's in public administration, Pritchett's in courts and their procedures, Truman's in political behavior and methodology.

In reply to queries about connections between philosophy and political science at Chicago, Harold Lasswell, Herman Pritchett, and Quincy Wright (who taught in the Political Science Department at Chicago from 1923 until 1956) all replied that they knew of no close relations between Merriam and any of the philosophers other than T. V. Smith. All three commented upon the considerable interdepartmental associations at Chicago, however. Lasswell said: "It must be remembered that the University of Chicago Faculty Club was very conveniently located and provided an easy means of continuing conversation that was rather fully taken advantage of." [54]

T. V. Smith was thought of as a political scientist as much as he was a philosopher. He came into the Chicago Philosophy Department as a graduate student in 1921 and was appointed an instructor in 1923. It was noted in Chapter I that Smith was not particularly close to any of the men under whom he studied. Smith himself took some pains in his autobiography to assert that, while he found his interests broadened by the study of pragmatism, he had reservations about the point of view. His comments on Ames, Mead, Moore, and Tufts are not entirely flattering. In fact, after calling Mead "the most stimulating intellectually" of the lot, he goes on to accuse Mead of confusion and obscurantism.[55] There seems no reason to doubt that the teachings of the pragmatists made little imprint on Smith's thinking. His political writings have a pragmatic tinge, but there is little concrete evidence in them of the problematic analysis of Mead, Dewey, Tufts, Moore, and Ames.

On their side, the Chicago philosophers remained interested in problems in sociology, economics, and politics, as Tufts indicated:

> Capitalism is on trial as to its ability to secure decent living conditions for all members of society. It is worth while to have an experiment which seeks to make sure of a minimum of necessities for all its citizens. Brutal as the rule of the Bolshevik has been in its methods of control, it has one principle which it may be well for the world to see tried under fair terms. The principle that all should share in at least the necessities is worth trying. At any rate, it is likely to have a considerable trial. The philosopher may be permitted to watch it, although he may expect in some quarters condemnation for his temerity. When the great world conducts a gigantic experiment, the philosopher may at least watch and learn.[56]

Cautious as this statement may be, it expresses the pragmatists' essential interest in social experiment as an instrument for the betterment of the conditions under which men live. That interest permeated the social disciplines that flourished at the University of Chicago during the time of the Chicago School. There were differences in the direction and in the mode of implementation of that interest among the departments concerned, but the important thing was the extent to which the usual walls between disciplines were broken down or ignored, to the mutual advantage of all the fields involved.

Wesley Mitchell, at the dedication of the university's Social Science Research Building in 1929, spoke of the guiding spirits at Chicago in his attempt to convince the social sciences that they had a common subject matter:

> It was impossible to fit Veblen into a department pigeonhole — he seemed to be economist, anthropologist, sociologist, social psychologist, and political scientist by turns. For his problem — how cumulative changes come about in social habits of thinking — is one which admits of no such sharp divisions as administrative convenience and the progress of specialization had raised within our universities. And Veblen's learning was wide enough to embrace those parts of all the social sciences which were most pertinent to his problem. One cannot understand the evolution of social institutions if he confines himself to any single specialty.
>
> With equal vigor John Dewey's philosophy called for co-operation among all the social sciences. . . . The old notion that a science like economics can borrow a few ready-made conclusions about human nature from psychology, and on this foundation erect

a towering theory of value and distribution, gave place to the realization that economics must recognize that it is a constructive study of human behavior, making its own peculiar contributions to the knowledge of social behavior. The like holds true of all the social sciences. They have a common problem and a common working program.[57]

VII

AFTERWORD · *Scholars and Community*

THE Chicago School was an academic phenomenon of a rare and important sort, whose like we will not see again soon. The combination of circumstances that brought about the phenomenon was not deliberately sought, as was pointed out in Chapter I. William Rainey Harper deservedly is credited with bringing the University of Chicago into being, but the mixture was not what he intended when he gathered the elements together. Instead of the traditional educational institution built around Semitics, classics, and philosophy that Harper had planned, Chicago began as a center of research in the natural and social sciences. When he could not get the seasoned men he wanted from Harvard and Johns Hopkins, he had to take a number whose reputations were still in the process of formation. Dewey was appointed only after the men Harper really wanted had turned him down. Veblen had to come as a student in order to get to Chicago, and he was barely tolerated after he became a member of the faculty. Men such as William I. Thomas, Frederick Starr, and Veblen did little to add to the traditional atmosphere Harper encouraged among his faculty, but they were the sort of maverick scholars who principally established the university's eminence. Also, the men who shaped the Philosophy Department and so much else at Chicago were not quite the venerable sages Harper had hoped for.

Moreover, in light of its ambitions, even worse than the effects of the unorthodox views of some of its faculty were the embarrassments the university suffered as a result of its religious and financial ties. The widespread skepticism in academic circles that a great university could grow under the tutelage of the Baptists, on the one hand, and of the arch-capitalist Rockefeller, on the other, kept Chicago on edge for quite a few years. It was a newcomer in a tradition-bound realm, without a niche into which it could fit with any comfort or assurance. Harper's efforts were creating an institution that fell somewhere between the staid ivy-covered halls of scholarship in the East and the great state universities of the Midwest. Trying to produce pure research and to shine in community service at the same time, the university was jumpy and watchful, characteristics that fortunately helped keep it alert and in ferment. That slight sense of insecurity and inferiority that so often marks the midwesterner, even when he is outdistancing his eastern or far-western counterpart, helped make for a spirit of comradeship on the campus. The fortuitous congregation of men eager for new ideas, in a cultural outpost with all the earmarks of a beleaguered garrison, resulted in an intellectual community of astounding power.

The emphasis should be on *community*. As James pointed out, there was intellect elsewhere—at Harvard, for instance; and there was community elsewhere—at Yale, as he said. But the intellectual activity in most instances was that of individuals who just happened to be in an academic setting, not that of members of a genuine community of inquiry. The communities that did exist, on the other hand, were comfortable bastions of philosophical conservatism, communal only in devotion to a common doctrine and in opposition to all threats to that doctrine. What was unique at Chicago was a conscious spirit of ground-breaking thought pervading the activities of an array of scholars in different fields who were interacting because of a common attitude toward inquiry and a common feeling of intellectual adventure.

The cooperative nature of research in the natural sciences is frequently overplayed. Yet there is a basis for the notion; the way in which some scientists, working from the same premises and toward similar goals, exchange data and experimental conclusions does represent intellectual cooperation. As anyone inside the profession knows, however, there also is considerable personal competition, protection of precious discoveries, and political maneuvering for status. But the fact remains that the amount of productive cooperation among scholars in the natural sciences outdistances anything of the kind in the social or human sciences. There are group projects galore in the social sciences, but projects usually externally shaped and hence not the focus for community. The University of Chicago in its early years did contain a community of scholars in the social studies. And perhaps the multifarious pressures on the new institution played a part in producing that community. If we take seriously the idea that intelligence and cooperation are products of shared troubled situations, threatening environments, as Dewey and Mead maintain, then the Chicago School and its related disciplines are dramatic exemplification of the theory they developed.

The heady atmosphere of those years could not last very long. The feeling of excitement and the sense of mission that bound so many together at Chicago depended upon a fortunate sequence of men and situations. There was Dewey, who in his person and functions tied together philosophy, psychology, and education. And although he was trying to juggle too many balls at once (which probably contributed to the sequence of events leading to his decision to leave Chicago), he made pragmatism, for many people, a remarkably fruitful way of looking at things. There was the Laboratory School, which provided a focal point for nearly all the men at Chicago who had an interest in education. There were the graduate students whose interests ranged widely and who carried messages from one field to another with disregard for discipline and department boundaries. And there was the university itself, self-conscious about its newness, its location in the hinterland, and its determination to achieve excellence. Just as the Laboratory School was set up to provide a microcosm of social organization and of social awareness, the University of Chicago itself provided on a larger scale a microcosm of the intellectual interrelatedness of the various social disciplines. But these connections that existed at Chicago for a time were unstable. They depended upon the force of individual men much more than upon institutional organization.

The professional pressures upon the men in any academic field of study come largely from outside the college or university in which those men happen to be functioning and in the long run will counter the integrative forces that may chance to exist in any one institution, unless that institution is able to develop strong integrative structures. The general education program in the undergraduate college at Chicago under Hutchins, for example, was just such an integrative academic structure. But as soon as Hutchins left Chicago, the pressures from the departments in the graduate schools began to undo that program. In much the same way, psychology pulled away from philosophy as soon as Dewey left Chicago, and functionalism tried to forget its origins. Cooperation between education and philosophy became less and less systematic and came to depend upon occasional cross-listed courses. The direct impact of philosophy upon sociology lasted as long as Mead did, but no longer. There were remnants of the spirit of the early days as late as the 1930's, but with the end of the Chicago School, the spirit was all but dead.

The spirit was possible because of an infectious awareness of related approaches to related problems. These approaches were truly scientific in imposing no formulas, presupposing no outcomes, and applying to a wide range of problems. Wesley Mitchell expressed well the sense of common endeavor in his remarks about how Dewey's discussions of logic were immediately relevant to Mitchell's interests in economics. The Chicago pragmatists developed a methodology that gave the social scientists at Chicago and elsewhere a frame of reference, a perspective, and a consciousness of continuity. It was a methodology that could not be erected legitimately into a fixed organon; it did not function to provide ready-made forms or languages to which social problems had to be adapted. If the character of the method were grasped at all, that method had to be used in such a way that the form and language grew out of the problem itself and reflected the peculiarities of that problem. Yet, at the same time, the interrelations among different social problems were retained through a common problematic perspective. Underlying the variety of problems social scientists faced could be seen the concept of the nature of action. The philosophic analysis of the act situation could serve as the base from which analysis of sociological or economic problems rose and to which proposed solutions were referred. It was that common frame of reference, then, that made it possible for discoveries in one field to be significant for inquiries in another field of human behavior.

The task of philosophy, on this view, was to develop the implications of the methodology and to apply that method to the realms of value: truth, beauty, and goodness. Therefore, philosophy could not be an isolated, technical discipline pursuing its private "philosophic" concerns. Philosophy had to look to psychology, sociology, economics, education, religion, etc. for the content of its own value problems, just as it had to count on those disciplines maintaining a connection with it. The key to the entire operation, of course, was a set of conditions conducive to the willingness of the men concerned to listen to what their colleagues in other departments were saying. Ideally, the outcome of such an openness among fields of study would be a continuing growth of all the inquiries involved, with the ongoing refinement of the method itself following from the results of its applications.

Dewey and Mead did keep their philosophies alive and growing to the very end, because they continued to inquire and to re-examine their ideas in the light of data, ideas, hypotheses, and questions from a variety of other fields. But neither of them later had anything like the fertile intellectual interactions of the early years. The effects of the loss of many of the external connections were more drastic in the cases of the men whose philosophies were less original than those of Dewey and Mead. None of the Chicago philosophers, however, was derivative to the extent of subordinating his philosophy to any special field of knowledge or of reducing it to an emotive or a logical residue left in the wake of the sciences. Philosophy remained for all of them a profound concern with how things *are* in the world. They knew that philosophic questions do not arise in a vacuum; those questions arise in intimate connection with the data, ideas, hypotheses, and questions growing out of the living processes of the world.

The Chicago philosophers knew enough about the processes of the world to avoid some of the more common errors of twentieth-century philosophy. Their reactions to the extremes of eighteenth- and nineteenth-century rationalisms did not push them to the opposite extreme. They recognized that the human situation is possible only for rational beings, but at the same time they saw that man is only partly and sporadically rational. Some of the positivists reverted to a practical irrationality, in the futile attempt to make philosophy conform to a very narrow conception of the physical sciences, with the strange result that logic was equated with philosophy, while ethics and aesthetics were banished to limbo. Certain existentialists, at the other extreme, tried to save men's rationality with respect to action and art, but they did so at the cost of disconnecting men from their environment and even from each other and relegating science to the realm of poetry.

Mead, Dewey, Tufts, and their colleagues developed a perspective within which they recognized the necessity for men to develop their powers of reason, even though reason is never entirely adequate to the problems that call it forth. Reason is a natural function of an organism at a certain level of complexity of interaction with its surroundings; and science, ethics, and art alike are products and characteristics of that functioning. Mead, especially, was long engaged in showing how human behavior, including that behavior we call intelligent, evolves out of more primitive, pre-human social situations to create natural valuings of all sorts. Moore drew the implications from this social analysis for the more special concerns of logic and metaphysics. Tufts, although his ethics centered on a self more than did that of the others, put that self into its historical and sociological setting and showed the role institutions play in guiding and limiting men's actions and hopes. Dewey, too, never lost sight of the social setting of the action that was the center of his interest. His emphasis was upon action, but his philosophy, in all its parts, must be read as presupposing the social ambient of action together with all the residual uncertainties inherent in that ambient, if that philosophy is to be seen as relevant to the problems to which Dewey addressed himself.

American psychology, in its determination to become a natural science, is not likely to ally itself openly with philosophy again soon; and that is probably just as well, in view of the dominant trends in philosophy at the moment. The vogue of philosophical psychology in England and on the Continent no doubt will spread in this country, but the American versions so far do not promise to prove much more useful to psychology proper than have the European versions. The great diversity among psychologists that exists today should produce valuable knowledge; and the more perceptive psychologists will come to see the restrictions put upon the discipline by too narrow outlooks and to see those paths that are leading to dead ends. If the time should come when psychologists have a conscious need for a broader, more philosophic orientation, a psychologist may well be one to work it out. Meanwhile, the broad-gauge behaviorisms of Dewey and Mead hold resources that may again be useful when that time arrives.

Education has become a center of general attention in the last few years, largely as a result of a growing realization that education is big business. As a consequence, the philosophy of education has become respectable again, and as one of the few modern philosophers who has worked out a theory of education, Dewey will remain a focal figure in this area for a long time to come. The real hope for education, however, will lie with men who retain the spirit of the efforts of Dewey and Mead to educate, rather than to train, people. In spite of flurries of interest in "new and experimental" modes of educating, our school systems have never absorbed the view of education as itself a problem-solving activity designed to promote intelligent habits of problem-solving. The new modes quickly become promotional gimmicks and unimaginative techniques clumsily applied. The role of the teacher, as the Chicago pragmatists saw it, requires a high degree of intelligence, a great deal of skill, and a firm sense of being a teacher and an inquirer rather than the traditional imparter of knowledge and trainer for examinations. It is likely that only a philosophy derived from an understanding of the social nature of men in the way the Chicago philosophy was will recognize the centrality of education to the entire human enterprise. As disciplines become esoteric in language and method and isolated in attention and bearing, the teacher withdraws from the scholar in self-defense and the scholar from the teacher in a false pose of superiority. From the pragmatic viewpoint, a teacher must also be a scholar, an inquirer into the learning process itself as well as into the subject matters taught. Similarly, a scholar, however lofty his researches, must maintain an awareness of the problems of communicating with others and of the effects of that communication upon them.

Many phases of Protestant religion in the United States bear the imprint of pragmatism. The imprint is of a general, rather vague pragmatic outlook, not the specific pragmatism of Dewey or Mead. There are followers of Dewey in religion and in religious education; but Dewey's views on religion, as noted above, are too anti-institutional to serve very directly in the solving of the problems faced by churches in a secular world. Ames does offer ideas for a solution to those problems — or at least for an approach to a solution — for churches. In the light of the growing movement for unification of Protestant sects, however, the utility of Ames's ideas is more likely to be recognized at the level of individual congregations than at the level of general church organization. For congregations, Ames's attempt to make religion natural, yet to keep it religious, is still relevant, particularly as an alternative to the neo-orthodoxies and the vulgarizations that pass as religious reformulations.

Sociologists are not as preoccupied with quantification as some of their fellows in other areas, although the sociology department of a large university recently refused admission to a graduate applicant because they considered his background too philosophic and they were bent upon becoming known as a "scientific" department. As the science of society, however, sociology will probably remain receptive to almost any useful generalizations about men and communities, even philosophic generalizations. And pragmatic concepts of the social and intellectual nature of men may have a renewed role in sociology through the influence of developments in anthropology. As theoretical accounts are developed in conjunction with more accurate observations of primate behavior, the analysis worked out by Dewey and, more especially, Mead may prove a starting point for further refinements in accounting for the emergence of language and intelligence.

Economics has become the most mathematical of the social sciences, and mathematics probably will be the dominant influence in the field for some time. Certainly most graduate study in the field is unlikely to produce another Veblen or Ayres. The fact remains, though, that economic problems are involved so thoroughly in the serious practical difficulties we face and will continue to face that some more broadly social view of economics is bound to survive, even if that view has to grow outside the strictly professional confines of the discipline of economics. And there is a budding renewal of interest in political economy, an interest which at least demonstrates a lingering awareness of the essential interconnections in our society among economics, politics, and ethics.

While political theory continues to be an acceptable area of concentration within the wider field of political science, philosophic thought about political action and institutions still will have a hearing. Dewey is respected as a leading philosopher of democracy, and his ideas should continue to enter into discussions of the aims and operations of political systems.

The most pertinent thing that the Chicago pragmatists still have to say to social scientists in general is precisely what they said to an earlier generation of social scientists. There seems to be a recurrent hope that if only the right formal structure can be found the social sciences will flower—enabling men to exercise the same sort of spectacular control over their social environment that they have gained over the physical environment. But one of the original goals of the Chicago philosophers was to show that fixed logics or fixed formal systems of any sort become strait-jackets instead of tools for inquiry. What they insisted upon was that logic and method should be instrumental to actual problems and that they should remain fluid in order to change with changing conditions of inquiry. The specific methodology of a particular social science ought to emerge out of the analysis of the basic kinds of problems that science embraces. If a mathematical language can be found for sociology, for instance, it is more likely to be found as a result of structural analogies between the mathematics and the conceptual structures worked out in the subject matter of sociology than to be discovered in independence of that subject matter.

Distortions always result when the materials of knowledge are forced into any mold brought in from outside the area of the materials themselves. Such distortions need not be particularly dangerous for science so long as the men employing them are conscious of the distortions and are prepared to modify or discard the molds when the use of them leads too far from the problematic situations themselves. Unfortunately, however, structures come to be valued in themselves because of a power of computation and a precision that are more apparent than real when tested against the experiential circumstances which the structures are supposed to clarify. Frank H. Knight has frequently pointed out to his fellow economists that the more mathematically precise they make their mathematical models, the farther they get from what actually transpires in the economic world.

The form and matter of a theory are abstractions from the process of inquiry, for the pragmatists, and method is an extracted set of guidelines for that inquiry. A general conception of method can be extracted from a general analysis of the process of inquiry. But form, matter, and method are all subject to growth and reform in the light of the ongoing procedure of inquiry itself. The realization of the ramifications of this pragmatic point of view can continue to be of value in a search for fruitful specialized approaches to social questions.

Moreover, both the social and natural sciences can learn something from the pragmatists' awareness that, no matter what degree of control we manage to attain over nature or society, control is never complete. Our attainments of goals are partial at best, and the goals themselves are subject to constant reassessment as we approach them. Our attempts at control for particular ends always produce unforeseen effects, some desirable and others highly undesirable, with the consequence that the control we do exercise may be bought at a price we are not really willing to pay—once we discover what the price is. Some (but not all) natural scientists are beginning to see the need for more caution in our search for and use of knowledge. The awareness of the inherent limitations on our ability to reach intended aims without introducing worse problems than those we solve would seem even more incumbent upon the social scientists bent upon social control. Dewey, Mead, Tufts, and Ames all tried to make clear the nature of experiments with societies, the necessity of continual alertness to all the indications available on whether action really is moving us toward desired goals, the importance of sensitivity to the full range of consequences of such experiment, and the requirement of conscious evaluation and re-evaluation of all we do in the light of actual consequences.

It would require a man of the ability, personality, and vision of Dewey or a man of the powerful intellect of Mead to make philosophy relevant once again to the spectrum of human concerns. And in order for that relevance to be recognized and utilized, there would have to be an array of intelligent, dynamic men susceptible to philosophic ideas similar to the array Dewey and Mead found at Chicago.

Angell, Moore, and Tufts have largely faded from the sight of all but a few historical scholars in psychology and philosophy. Ames will be memorialized in his church for a while to come. Dewey and Mead are becoming classic figures of American thought, celebrated in scholarly articles and books and tucked away into convenient slots for ready reference. The example of these men serves mainly as a source of wonder; we know very little about how to go about instituting a scholarly community—instituting communication among men whose research is various but whose feeling of a common scholarly venture is kept alive by genuine interaction of ideas.

Before we can deliberately construct another such enterprise as the Chicago School was for a few years, our educators will have to learn to inculcate the spirit of cooperative inquiry instead of competitive amassing of facts and taking of tests that characterize most instruction. Somehow or other, some aesthetic or ethical or scientific value will have to gain at least equal status in our culture with the profit motive. Meanwhile, the burst of energy and productivity and the impetus in curiosity and morale produced in such a short period at Chicago by a group of industrious, open-minded scholars willing to ignore party and department lines gives us a glimpse of what an intellectual community might be. An institution that produced acknowledged schools of philosophy, psychology, education, religion, sociology, and political science should stand as an assurance that willingness to talk — and to listen — across academic barriers need not contaminate the disciplines concerned but may even strengthen and invigorate them. Our studies may be broken into bits and pieces, but knowledge that deserves the name is continuous with all other knowledge (or can be made so). The notion that all we know and do and feel rises out of action is still a promising start for realizing that continuity and for trying to make real a wholeness in our knowledge and our lives.

The social sciences need to be reminded periodically of Dewey's observation in *Experience and Nature*: "The world seems mad in pre-occupation with what is specific, particular, disconnected in medicine, politics, science, industry, education. In terms of a conscious control of inclusive wholes, search for those links which occupy key positions and which effect critical connections is indispensable. But recovery of sanity depends upon seeing and using these specifiable things *as* links functionally significant in a process." [1] For, as the Chicago philosophers saw, the social sciences are the proper (and most likely) instruments for putting the abstracted connections discovered by the natural sciences into human perspective for human use. The urgency of some such realization in politics and education has not diminished since Dewey voiced the need. And while, as with any philosophy, some of the details of fact and accepted theory may have changed since this pragmatism was worked out, the basic structure of the philosophy – its principles, its attitudes, and its method – stands as a possible source of direction and insight for those disciplines upon which it had such a salutary effect during its formative years.

Notes

NOTES

I. INTRODUCTION

1 *Letters of William James* (Boston: Atlantic Monthly Press, 1920), II, 201–2. Letter to Mrs. Henry Whitman.

2 William James, "The Chicago School," *Psychological Bulletin*, 1 (no. 1):1 (January 15, 1904). John Dewey *et al.*, *Studies in Logical Theory* (Chicago: University of Chicago Press, 1903).

3 John Dewey, *Essays in Experimental Logic* (Chicago: University of Chicago Press, 1916), p. 347; reissued by Dover, New York, in 1953.

4 Thomas W. Goodspeed, *A History of the University of Chicago* (Chicago: University of Chicago Press, 1916), pp. 130–31.

5 *The President's Report; The Decennial Publications of the University of Chicago*, First Series, I (Chicago: University of Chicago Press, 1903), p. xviii.

6 Goodspeed, *A History of the University of Chicago*, p. 211.

7 Letter from Tufts to Harper, no date, in the Archives of the University of Chicago. Quoted by Robert L. McCaul in "A Preliminary Listing of Dewey Letters, 1894–1904," *School and Society*, 87 (no. 2159):399 (October 10, 1959).

8 Goodspeed, *A History of the University of Chicago*, p. 97.

9 J. M. Powis Smith, "President Harper: Scholar and Creator," *University Record (Chicago)*, 18 (no. 3):169 (July 1932).

10 Letter from Dewey to Harper, April 28, 1897, in the University of Chicago Archives.

11 Edward S. Ames, *Beyond Theology: The Autobiography of Edward Scribner Ames*, ed. Van Meter Ames (Chicago: University of Chicago Press, 1959), p. 52.

12 Katherine C. Mayhew and Anna C. Edwards, *The Dewey School* (New York: D. Appleton-Century, 1936), p. 10; reissued by Atherton Press, New York, in 1966.

13 Marion Talbot, "The Challenge of a Retrospect," *University Record (Chicago)*, 11 (no. 2):87 (April 1925).

14 Shailer Mathews, "Speech at the Trustees' Dinner," *University Record (Chicago)*, 19 (no. 2):113 (April 1933).

15 Quoted in W. Carson Ryan, *Studies in Early Graduate Education: The Johns Hopkins, Clark University, the University of Chicago* (New York: Carnegie Foundation for the Advancement of Teaching, 1939), p. 106.

16 Letters from Dwight to Harper in 1890 quoted in *ibid.*, p. 108.

17 G. Stanley Hall, *Life and Confessions of a Psychologist* (New York: D. Appleton, 1923), pp. 295–97.

18 *New York Evening Post*, October 5, 1895. Quoted in Joseph Dorfman, *Thorstein Veblen and His America* (New York: Viking Press, 1934), p. 122.

19 *American Journal of Sociology*, 1 (no. 2):210 (September 1895).

20 Ryan, *Studies in Early Graduate Education*, p. 127.

21 Letter from Lester F. Ward to Mrs. J. O. Unger, April 1, 1905, quoted in Dorfman, *Thorstein Veblen*, p. 255.

22 Mayhew and Edwards discuss in *The Dewey School* some of the school's financial problems. See also Robert L. McCaul, "Dewey and the University of Chicago," *School and Society*, 89 (no. 2189):153ff (March 25, 1961).

23 George H. Mead, *The Philosophy of the Present* (Chicago: Open Court, 1932); *Mind, Self and Society* (Chicago: University of Chicago Press, 1934); *Movements of Thought in the Nineteenth Century* (Chicago: University of Chicago Press, 1936); *The Philosophy of the Act* (Chicago: University of Chicago Press, 1938).

24 John Dewey, "George Herbert Mead," *Journal of Philosophy*, 28 (no. 12):310–11 (June 4, 1931).

25 *Ibid.*, p. 310.

26 James H. Tufts, "On the Genesis of the Aesthetic Categories," in *Investigations Representing the Departments; The Decennial Publications of the University of Chicago*, First Series, III, Part 2 (Chicago: University of Chicago Press, 1903), pp. 5–12.

27 James H. Tufts, "Can Epistemology Be Based on Mental States?" *Philosophical Review*, 6 (no. 6):577–92 (November 1897).

28 James H. Tufts, "Ethical Value," *Journal of Philosophy, Psychology, and Scientific Methods*, 5 (no. 19):517–22 (September 10, 1908); "The Present Task of Ethical Theory," *International Journal of Ethics*, 20 (no. 2):141–52 (January 1910); and "The Moral Life and the Construction of Values and Standards," in John Dewey *et al.*, *Creative Intelligence* (New York: Henry Holt, 1917).

29 John Dewey and James H. Tufts, *Ethics*, 1st ed. (New York: Henry Holt, 1908); 2nd ed. (New York: Henry Holt, 1932).

30 John Dewey, "Religious Education as Conditioned by Modern Psychology and Pedagogy," in *The Religious Education Association: Proceedings of the First Annual Convention* (Chicago: Executive Office of the Association, 1903), pp. 60–66.

31 Matilde Castro Tufts, "Addison W. Moore as Teacher," *University Record (Chicago)*, 17 (no. 1):49–50 (January 1931).

32 George H. Mead, "Dr. Moore's Philosophy," *University Record (Chicago)*, 17 (no. 1):48 (January 1931).

33 Ames, *Beyond Theology*, p. 44.

34 Paul Shorey, "The Spirit of the University of Chicago," *University of Chicago Magazine*, 1 (no. 6):242 (April 1909).

II. PHILOSOPHY

1 James R. Angell, "The Relations of Structural and Functional Psychology to Philosophy," in *Investigations Representing the Departments; The*

Decennial Publications of the University of Chicago, First Series, III, Part 2 (Chicago: University of Chicago Press, 1903), pp. 66, 67, 69, 73.

2 James R. Angell, *Psychology*, 1st ed. (New York: Henry Holt, 1904), p. 9.

3 Addison W. Moore, "Existence, Meaning, and Reality in Locke's Essay and in Present Epistemology," *Investigations Representing the Departments; Decennial Publications*, First Series, III, Part 2, pp. 40–41.

4 John Dewey, "Thought and Its Subject Matter: The General Problem of Logical Theory," in Dewey *et al.*, *Studies in Logical Theory* (Chicago: University of Chicago Press, 1903), pp. 14–16. This point of view is said to have been derived from Trendelenburg by way of George S. Morris. See Gershon Rosenstock, *F. A. Trendelenburg: Forerunner to John Dewey* (Carbondale: Southern Illinois University Press, 1964).

5 Dewey, "Thought and Its Subject Matter: The General Problem of Logical Theory," in Dewey *et al.*, *Studies in Logical Theory*, p. 14n; Addison W. Moore, "Some Logical Aspects of Purpose," *ibid.*, p. 345n.

6 See "Studies from the Psychological Laboratory of the University of Chicago," *Psychological Review*, 3(no. 3):245–58, 258–69 (May 1896); 3(no. 4):371–77, 378–83 (July 1896); 5(no. 6):579–95, 595–615 (November 1898).

7 John Dewey, *Psychology* (New York: Harper and Brothers, 1887); reissued in Dewey, *The Early Works, 1882–1898*: Vol. 2, 1887, *Psychology* (Carbondale and Edwardsville: Southern Illinois Press, 1967).

8 John Dewey, "The Psychological Standpoint," *Mind*, 11(no. 41):1–19 (January 1886); "Psychology as Philosophic Method," *Mind*, 11(no. 42):153–73 (April 1886); both articles are reprinted in John Dewey, *Philosophy, Psychology, and Social Practice*, ed. Joseph Ratner (New York: G. P. Putnam's Sons, 1963).

9 Moore, in *Investigations Representing the Departments; Decennial Publications*, First Series, III, Part 2, p. 41n.

10 George H. Mead, "Suggestions toward a Theory of the Philosophical Disciplines," *Philosophical Review*, 9(no. 1):1–17 (January 1900); reprinted in Mead, *Selected Writings*, ed. Andrew J. Reck (Indianapolis: Bobbs-Merrill, 1964).

11 John Dewey, "The Reflex Arc Concept in Psychology," *Psychological Review*, 3(no. 4):357–70 (July 1896). This article is frequently mentioned as the foundation of functional psychology, and it served as a basic reference for almost all the men of the Chicago School. Dewey's "The Theory of Emotion," *Psychological Review*, 1(no. 6):553–69 (November 1894), 2(no. 1):13–32 (January 1895), had in part anticipated the basic position of the 1896 article. Both articles are reprinted in Dewey, *Philosophy, Psychology, and Social Practice.*

12 John Dewey, *How We Think* (Boston: D. C. Heath, 1910).

13 James R. Angell, *Chapters from Modern Psychology* (New York: Longmans, Green, 1912), p. 4.

14 James R. Angell, *An Introduction to Psychology* (New York: Henry Holt, 1918), p. 8.

15 John Dewey, "Green's Theory of the Moral Motive," *Philosophical Review*, 1(no. 6):597 (November 1892). This view, again, has been attributed to Trendelenburg. See note 4.

16 Moore, in *Investigations Representing the Departments; Decennial Publications*, First Series, III, Part 2, p. 47.

17 Moore, "Some Logical Aspects of Purpose," in Dewey *et al.*, *Studies in Logical Theory*, p. 382.

18 See especially John Dewey, " 'Consciousness' and Experience," in *The Influence of Darwin on Philosophy* (New York: Henry Holt, 1910), and his essays in Dewey *et al.*, *Studies in Logical Theory*; also James H. Tufts, "Can Epistemology Be Based on Mental States?" *Philosophical Review*, 6(no. 6): 577–92 (November 1897).

19 John Dewey, "Thought and Its Subject Matter: The Content and Object of Thought," in Dewey *et al.*, *Studies in Logical Theory*, p. 81n.

20 John Dewey, "The Postulate of Immediate Empiricism," *The Influence of Darwin on Philosophy*, p. 227.

21 George H. Mead, *The Philosophy of the Act* (Chicago: University of Chicago Press, 1938), p. 112.

22 George H. Mead, "The Philosophical Basis of Ethics," *International Journal of Ethics*, 18(no. 3):314 (April 1908); reprinted in Mead, *Selected Writings*.

23 Mead, *The Philosophy of the Act*, pp. 26–44.

24 Dewey, "Thought and Its Subject Matter: The General Problem of Logical Theory," in Dewey *et al.*, *Studies in Logical Theory*, p. 19.

25 Angell, *Psychology*, 1st ed., p. 1.

26 William James, *The Principles of Psychology* (New York: Henry Holt, 1910), I, 183–85.

27 Dewey, "The Reflex Arc Concept in Psychology," *Psychological Review*, 3:368. See also Angell, *Psychology*, 1st ed., pp. 50–52; 4th ed. (New York: Henry Holt, 1908), pp. 63–64.

28 Moore, in *Investigations Representing the Departments; Decennial Publications*, First Series, III, Part 2, pp. 41–43.

29 See John Dewey, "The Theory of Emotions (II)," *Psychological Review*, 2:32, and George H. Mead, *Mind, Self and Society* (Chicago: University of Chicago Press, 1934), pp. 16–18.

30 Myron L. Ashley, "The Nature of Hypothesis," in Dewey *et al.*, *Studies in Logical Theory*, p. 154.

31 John Dewey, *Outlines of a Critical Theory of Ethics* (Ann Arbor, Mich.: Register Publishing Co., 1891), p. 1; reprinted in 1957 by Hillary House in New York. See also John Dewey and James H. Tufts, *Ethics*, 1st ed. (New York: Henry Holt, 1908), p. 1.

32 Henry W. Stuart, "Valuation as a Logical Process," in Dewey *et al.*, *Studies in Logical Theory*, pp. 237–40; Mead, "The Philosophical Basis of Ethics," *International Journal of Ethics*, 18:312–13; James H. Tufts, "The Moral Life and the Construction of Values and Standards," in John Dewey *et al.*, *Creative Intelligence* (New York: Henry Holt, 1917), pp. 358–63.

33 Stuart, "Valuation as a Logical Process," in Dewey *et al.*, *Studies in Logical Theory*, pp. 237–38.

34 Charles Morris, Introduction to Mead, *Mind, Self and Society*, p. xxxi.

35 William James, *The Will to Believe and Other Essays in Popular Philosophy* (New York: Longmans, Green, 1897), pp. 184–210.

36 Mead, "Suggestions toward a Theory of the Philosophical Disciplines," *Philosophical Review*, 9:14–15.

37 Mead, *Mind, Self and Society*, p. 386.

38 *Ibid.*

39 Mead, *The Philosophy of the Act*, pp. 464, 465.

40 John Dewey, "Self-Realization as the Moral Ideal," *Philosophical Review*, 2(no. 6):664 (November 1893). See also Mead, *Mind, Self and Society*, p. 385; and Dewey and Tufts, *Ethics*, 1st ed., p. 284.

41 See Dewey, *Outlines of a Critical Theory of Ethics*, pp. 216–17, and "Self-Realization as the Moral Ideal," *Philosophical Review*, 2:661; Dewey and Tufts, *Ethics*, 1st ed., pp. 364–66; and Mead, "Suggestions toward a Theory of the Philosophical Disciplines," *Philosophical Review*, 9:15–16.

42 Addison W. Moore, "Reformation of Logic," in Dewey *et al.*, *Creative Intelligence*, p. 84.

43 Addison W. Moore, "Absolutism and Teleology," *Philosophical Review*, 18(no. 3):317 (May 1909).

44 Dewey, *Outlines of a Critical Theory of Ethics*, p. 206.

45 Mead, *The Philosophy of the Act*, pp. 460–61.

46 Mead, *Mind, Self and Society*, p. 384.

47 Stuart, "Valuation as a Logical Process," in Dewey *et al.*, *Studies in Logical Theory*, p. 300.

48 Dewey, *Outlines of a Critical Theory of Ethics*, pp. 135–36.

49 See Stuart, "Valuation as a Logical Process," in Dewey *et al.*, *Studies in Logical Theory*, p. 293; Mead, *The Philosophy of the Act*, pp. 461–65, and "Scientific Method and the Moral Sciences," *International Journal of Ethics*, 33(no. 3):242–43 (April 1923), reprinted in Mead, *Selected Writings*; John Dewey, "Progress," *International Journal of Ethics*, 26(no. 3):314–15 (April 1916); Moore, in Dewey *et al.*, *Creative Intelligence*, pp. 98–99.

50 Moore, "Absolutism and Teleology," *Philosophical Review*, 18:313.

51 John Dewey, *The Ethics of Democracy* (Ann Arbor: Andrews, 1888), p. 22.

52 Mead, "Scientific Method and the Moral Sciences," *International Journal of Ethics*, 33:238–39.

53 Dewey, *Outlines of a Critical Theory of Ethics*, p. 121.

54 James H. Tufts, "On the Genesis of the Aesthetic Categories," in *Investigations Representing the Departments; Decennial Publications*, First Series, III, Part 2, pp. 8–11.

55 John Dewey, *The School and Society* (Chicago: University of Chicago Press, 1900), pp. 103–4. See also *Outlines of a Critical Theory of Ethics*, pp. 120–23.

56 George H. Mead, "The Nature of Aesthetic Experience," *International Journal of Ethics*, 36(no. 4):387 (July 1926); reprinted in Mead, *Selected Writings*. All the points mentioned here are developed in detail by Dewey in *Art as Experience* (New York: Minton, Balch, 1934).

57 Mead, "Suggestions toward a Theory of the Philosophical Disciplines," *Philosophical Review*, 9:17.

58 Tufts, "Can Epistemology Be Based on Mental States?" *Philosophical Review*, 6:592.

59 Dewey, *Outlines of a Critical Theory of Ethics*, pp. 224–25; Mead, *The Philosophy of the Act*, pp. 466–74.

60 Angell, *Psychology*, 1st ed., pp. 242–44; 4th ed., pp. 287–88.

61 Mead, *The Philosophy of the Act*, p. 83; see also Mead, "Suggestions toward a Theory of the Philosophical Disciplines," *Philosophical Review*, 9:5; and Stuart, "Valuation as a Logical Process," in Dewey *et al.*, *Studies in Logical Theory*, p. 239.

62 Ashley, "The Nature of Hypothesis," in Dewey *et al.*, *Studies in Logical Theory*.

63 *Ibid.*, pp. 174–75; Dewey, *How We Think*, pp. 88–90.

64 Addison W. Moore, *Pragmatism and Its Critics* (Chicago: University of Chicago Press, 1910), p. 19.

65 John Dewey, "Is Logic a Dualistic Science?" *Open Court*, 3 (no. 47): 2041 (January 16, 1890).

66 John Dewey, "Thought and Its Subject Matter: The Antecedent Conditions and Cues of the Thought-Function," in Dewey *et al.*, *Studies in Logical Theory*, p. 23. By "characteristic functions and attitudes," he means such as the technological, aesthetic, religious, scientific, socioethical. See *ibid.*, p. 18.

67 Dewey, *How We Think*, p. 72.

68 Mead, *Mind, Self and Society*, p. 71. On the question of meaning and of truth, see Dewey's essays in *Studies in Logical Theory*, pp. 33–34, 66–85, and Moore, in *Investigations Representing the Departments; Decennial Publications*, First Series, III, Part 2, pp. 41–51.

69 Moore, in Dewey *et al.*, *Creative Intelligence*, pp. 84–85.

70 George H. Mead, "Doctor Moore's Philosophy," *University Record (Chicago)*, 17 (no. 1):48–49 (January 1931).

III. PSYCHOLOGY

1 John Dewey, "The New Psychology," *Andover Review*, 2 (no. 9):285 (September 1884).

2 John Dewey, "The Psychological Standpoint," *Mind*, 11 (no. 41):1–19 (January 1886) and "Psychology as Philosophic Method," *Mind*, 11 (no. 42): 153–73 (April 1886).

3 John Dewey, *Psychology*, 3rd rev. ed. (New York: American Book, 1891), pp. 43–44.

4 John Dewey, "Is Logic a Dualistic Science?" *Open Court*, 3 (no. 47): 2041 (January 16, 1890).

5 John Dewey, "From Absolutism to Experimentalism," in *Contemporary American Philosophy: Personal Statements*, ed. George P. Adams and William Pepperell Montague (New York: Macmillan, 1930), II, 23–25; reprinted in *John Dewey on Experience, Nature, and Freedom*, ed. Richard J. Bernstein (New York: Liberal Arts, 1960).

6 George H. Mead, "Herr Lasswitz on Energy and Epistemology," *Psychological Review*, 1 (no. 2):175 (March 1894). Dewey compares the change in tensions in a psychological event to that of a physical process in "The Reflex Arc Concept," *Psychological Review*, 3 (no. 4):364 (July 1896).

7 John Dewey, "The Theory of Emotion. (I) Emotional Attitudes," *Psychological Review*, 1 (no. 6):564 (November 1894).

8 John Dewey, "The Theory of Emotion. (II) The Significance of Emotions," *Psychological Review*, 2 (no. 1):18–19, 25 (January 1895). Simon F. McLennan stated a similar theory of emotion in "Emotion, Desire and Interest: Descriptive," *Psychological Review*, 2 (no. 5):462–74 (September 1895).

9 James R. Angell and Addison W. Moore, "Reaction-Time: A Study in Attention and Habit," *Psychological Review*, 3 (no. 3):253 (May 1896).

10 Dewey, "The Theory of Emotion (I)," *Psychological Review*, 1:568n.

11 James R. Angell, "The Province of Functional Psychology," *Psychological Review*, n.s., 14(no. 2):83 (March 1907).

12 E. B. Titchener, "The Postulates of a Structural Psychology," *Philosophical Review*, 7(no. 5):453 (September 1898).

13 E. B. Titchener, "Structural and Functional Psychology," *Philosophical Review*, 8(no. 3):291 (May 1899). Later, Titchener joined forces with Angell in common opposition to the behaviorism of Watson. See Titchener, "On 'Psychology as the Behaviorist Views It,'" *Proceedings of the American Philosophical Society*, 53(no. 213):1–17 (January–May 1914).

14 George H. Mead, "The Definition of the Psychical," in *Investigations Representing the Departments; The Decennial Publications of the University of Chicago*, First Series, III, Part 2 (1903), pp. 77–112; reprinted in Mead, *Selected Writings*, ed. Andrew J. Reck (Indianapolis: Bobbs-Merrill, 1964).

15 *Ibid*., p. 109.

16 *Ibid*., pp. 107–8.

17 *Ibid*., p. 109.

18 Dewey, "The Theory of Emotion (I)," *Psychological Review*, 1:555.

19 Dewey, "The Theory of Emotion (II)," *Psychological Review*, 2:30.

20 James R. Angell, "The Influence of Darwin on Psychology," *Psychological Review*, n.s., 16 (no. 3): 152–69 (May 1909).

21 James R. Angell, *An Introduction to Psychology* (New York: Henry Holt, 1918), p. 209.

22 Harvey Carr, *Psychology* (New York: Longmans, Green, 1925).

23 See Angell's general statement of this conception of consciousness: *Psychology*, 1st ed. (New York: Henry Holt, 1904), p. 50; 4th ed. (New York: Henry Holt, 1908), pp. 63–64.

24 Dewey, "The Reflex Arc Concept," *Psychological Review*, 3:368. See also Angell, *Psychology*, 1st ed., pp. 116–18; 4th ed., pp. 148–49.

25 Sidney Ratner and Jules Altman, eds., *John Dewey and Arthur F. Bentley: A Philosophical Correspondence, 1932–1951* (New Brunswick, N.J.: Rutgers University Press, 1964), p. 53.

26 John Dewey, "Conduct and Experience," in *Psychologies of 1930*, ed. Carl Murchison (Worcester, Mass.: Clark University Press, 1930), pp. 410, 413–14.

27 James R. Angell, in *A History of Psychology in Autobiography*, ed. Carl Murchison (Worcester, Mass.: Clark University Press, 1936), III, 21–22.

28 James R. Angell and Simon F. McLennan, "The Organic Effects of Agreeable and Disagreeable Stimuli," *Psychological Review*, 3(no. 4):371–77 (July 1896).

29 James R. Angell and Helen B. Thompson, "A Study of the Relations between Certain Organic Processes and Consciousness," *Psychological Review*, 6(no. 1):32–69 (January 1899).

30 James R. Angell and Warner Fite, "The Monaural Localization of Sound," *Psychological Review*, 8(no. 3):225–46 (May 1901), and James R. Angell, "A Preliminary Study of the Significance of Partial Tones in the Localization of Sound," *Psychological Review*, 10(no. 1):1–14 (January 1903).

31 John B. Watson, in Murchison, ed., *A History of Psychology in Autobiography*, III, p. 274.

32 *Ibid*., p. 273.

33 John B. Watson, *Psychology from the Standpoint of a Behaviorist*, 2nd ed. (Philadelphia: J. B. Lippincott, 1924), p. viii.

34 James R. Angell, "Behavior as a Category of Psychology," *Psychological Review*, 20(no. 4):255–70 (July 1913).

35 Watson, in Murchison, ed., *A History of Psychology in Autobiography*, III, p. 281.

36 Watson, *Psychology from the Standpoint of a Behaviorist*, p. vii.

37 Harvey Carr, in Murchison, ed., *A History of Psychology in Autobiography*, III, pp. 80–81.

38 James R. Angell, *Chapters from Modern Psychology* (New York: Longmans, Green, 1912).

39 Carr, *Psychology*, p. 1.

40 *Ibid.*, p. 68.

41 *Ibid.*, pp. 68–69.

42 *Ibid.*, p. 69.

43 *Ibid.*, p. 76.

44 Charles H. Judd, *Psychology: General Introduction* (New York: Charles Scribner's Sons, 1907), p. v.

45 *Ibid.*, p. 22.

46 *Ibid.*, pp. 131–32.

47 *Ibid.*, p. 212.

48 Charles H. Judd, *The Psychology of Social Institutions* (New York: Macmillan, 1927).

49 Charles H. Judd, *Educational Psychology* (Boston: Houghton Mifflin, 1939).

50 James H. Tufts, *America's Social Morality* (New York: Henry Holt, 1933), pp. 195, 213.

51 Edna Heidbreder, *Seven Psychologies* (New York: Century, 1933), pp. 230–31.

52 John Dewey, *Human Nature and Conduct* (New York: Henry Holt, 1922), p. 153; reissued with new introduction by the Modern Library, New York, in 1930.

53 John Dewey, *The Sources of a Science of Education* (New York: Horace Liveright, 1929), pp. 68–70.

54 James R. Angell, in Murchison, ed., *A History of Psychology in Autobiography*, III, p. 37.

55 Angell, *Introduction to Psychology*, pp. 250–51.

56 Angell, *Psychology*, 1st ed., p. 305; 4th ed., p. 358.

57 Watson, *Psychology from the Standpoint of a Behaviorist*, p. xii.

58 Carr, in Murchison, ed., *A History of Psychology in Autobiography*, III, pp. 81–82.

59 Watson, *Psychology from the Standpoint of a Behaviorist*, p. vii.

60 John Dewey, "Ethics," *The Encyclopedia Americana* (1904).

61 James H. Tufts, "Psychological Literature: Social Psychology," *Psychological Review*, 2(no. 3):308 (May 1895).

62 John Dewey, "The Significance of the Problem of Knowledge," in *The Influence of Darwin on Philosophy* (New York: Henry Holt, 1910), p. 302.

63 George H. Mead, Review of C. L. Morgan, *An Introduction to Comparative Psychology*, *Psychological Review*, 2(no. 4):401 (July 1895).

64 George H. Mead, "The Genesis of the Self and Social Control," *Inter-*

national Journal of Ethics, 35(no. 3):253–54 (April 1925); reprinted in Mead, *Selected Writings*.

65 George H. Mead, "Social Psychology as Counterpart to Physiological Psychology," *Psychological Bulletin*, 6(no. 12):402 (December 15, 1909); reprinted in Mead, *Selected Writings*.

66 *Ibid*., p. 403.

67 *Ibid*., pp. 404–7.

68 George H. Mead, *Mind, Self and Society* (Chicago: University of Chicago Press, 1934), pp. 2–13.

69 *Ibid*., pp. 7–8.

70 John B. Watson, *Behaviorism* (New York: W. W. Norton, 1924), p. 17.

71 George H. Mead, "Concerning Animal Perception," *Psychological Review*, 14(no. 6):383–90 (November 1907); reprinted in Mead, *Selected Writings*.

72 Mead, "Suggestions toward a Theory of the Philosophical Disciplines," *Philosophical Review*, 9(no. 1):5–9 (January 1900).

73 Mead, "Concerning Animal Perception," *Psychological Review*, 14:387.

74 Mead, *Mind, Self and Society*, pp. 6–7.

IV. EDUCATION

1 Isaac L. Kandel, *American Education in the Twentieth Century* (Cambridge, Mass.: Harvard University Press, 1957), p. 137.

2 Merle Curti, *The Social Ideas of American Educators* (New York: Charles Scribner's Sons, 1935), pp. 379–85.

3 Robert L. McCaul, "Dewey's Chicago," *School Review*, 67(no. 2):269–72 (Summer 1959).

4 John Dewey, "How Much Freedom in New Schools?" *New Republic*, 63(no. 814):204 (July 9, 1930).

5 Ida Cass Heffron, *Francis Wayland Parker* (Los Angeles: Ivan Deach, Jr., 1934), p. 36.

6 John Dewey, *The School and Society* (Chicago: University of Chicago Press, 1900), author's note.

7 *Ibid*., pp. 115–25.

8 "An Unpublished Paper by George Herbert Mead," introduction by Darnell Rucker, *School and Society*, 96(no. 2304):151 (March 2, 1968).

9 George H. Mead, "The Teaching of Science in College," *Science*, n.s., 24(no. 613):395 (September 28, 1906); reprinted in Mead, *Selected Writings*, ed. Andrew J. Reck (Indianapolis: Bobbs-Merrill, 1964). See also John Dewey and Evelyn Dewey, *Schools of Tomorrow* (New York: E. P. Dutton, 1915), p. 13.

10 "An Unpublished Paper by George Herbert Mead," *School and Society*, 96:149.

11 *Ibid*., p. 151.

12 John Dewey, *The Child and the Curriculum* (Chicago: University of Chicago Press, 1902).

13 John Dewey, "The Psychological Aspect of the School Curriculum," *Educational Review*, 13:368 (April 1897).

14 John Dewey, "The Primary-Education Fetich," reprinted from *Forum*,

25(no. 3):315–28 (May 1898), in *Education Today* (New York: G. P. Putnam's Sons, 1940), p. 26.

15 *Ibid.*, pp. 24–25.

16 *Ibid.*, pp. 26–27.

17 George H. Mead, "The Psychology of Social Consciousness Implied in Instruction," *Science*, 31(no. 801):688–93 (May 6, 1910); reprinted in Mead, *Selected Writings*.

18 Dewey, "The Psychological Aspect of the School Curriculum," *Educational Review*, 13:368–69.

19 Dewey and Dewey, *Schools of Tomorrow*, pp. 137–38.

20 Dewey, *The School and Society*, pp. 27–28.

21 Mead, "The Psychology of Social Consciousness Implied in Instruction," *Science*, 31:690.

22 Ira W. Howerth, "The Social Aim in Education," in *The Fifth Yearbook of the National Herbart Society* (Chicago: University of Chicago Press, 1899), p. 108. The essay is taken from Howerth's Ph.D. thesis.

23 Albion Small, "Some Demands of Sociology upon Pedagogy," *American Journal of Sociology*, 2(no. 6):839 (May 1896).

24 John Dewey, *My Pedagogic Creed* (New York: E. L. Kellogg, 1897), p. 7; reprinted in *Dewey on Education*, with introduction and notes by Martin S. Dworkin (New York: Bureau of Publications, Columbia University Teachers College, 1959). See also Dewey, *The School and Society*, pp. 90–91, and *Democracy and Education* (New York: Macmillan, 1916), p. 117.

25 George H. Mead, "Educational Aspects of Trade Schools," *Union Labor Advocate*, 8(no. 7):19–20 (1908). See also James H. Tufts, "Editorial Notes," *School Review*, 14(no. 7):535–37 (September 1906).

26 *A Report on Vocational Training in Chicago and in Other Cities*, by Committee of the City Club, George H. Mead, Chairman (Chicago: City Club of Chicago, 1912). Quoted from Mead's typescript in the Department of Philosophy, University of Chicago.

27 George H. Mead, "Editorial Notes," *Elementary School Teacher*, 9(no. 3):156–57 (November 1908).

28 John Dewey, *Moral Principles in Education* (Boston: Houghton Mifflin, 1909), p. 32; reissued in a facsimile edition by Philosophical Library, New York, 1959.

29 John Dewey, "Democracy in Education," *Elementary School Teacher*, 4(no. 4):200 (December 1903).

30 *Ibid.*, p. 193.

31 See especially Dewey's "Interest in Relation to Training of the Will," in *Second Supplement to the Herbart Yearbook for 1895* (Chicago: University of Chicago Press, 1899); reprinted in *Educational Essays* (London: Blackie and Son, 1910). See also Dewey, "The Psychological Aspect of the School Curriculum," *Educational Review*, 13:356–58.

32 James H. Tufts, "How Far Is Formal Systematic Instruction Desirable in Moral Training in the Schools?" *Religious Education*, 3(no. 4): 121–25 (October 1908); "The Problem of Moral Education in the Public Schools as Affected by the Changed Conditions in Industry and Home Life," *Religious Education*, 4(no. 5):343–48 (October 1909); "The Teaching of Ideals," *School Review*, 22(no. 5):326–33 (May 1914); "Ethics in High Schools and Colleges," *Religious Education*, 9(no. 5):454–59 (October 1914).

33 Tufts, "How Far Is Formal Systematic Instruction Desirable in Moral Training in the Schools?" *Religious Education*, 3:123–24.
34 Tufts, "The Teaching of Ideals," *School Review*, 22:326–30.
35 *Ibid.*, p. 332.
36 James H. Tufts, *The Ethics of Coöperation* (Boston: Houghton Mifflin, 1918), p. 5.
37 Dewey, *Moral Principles in Education*, pp. 24–25.
38 John Dewey, "Religion and Our Schools," *Hibbert Journal*, 6(no. 4): 796–809 (July 1908); reprinted in *Intelligence in the Modern World*, ed. Joseph Ratner (New York: Modern Library, 1939), pp. 702–15.
39 John Dewey, "The Chaos in Moral Training," *Popular Science Monthly*, 45(no. 33):441 (August 1894).
40 George H. Mead, undated, untitled fragment, Archives of the University of Chicago.
41 John Dewey, "Culture and Industry in Education," *Educational Bi-Monthly*, 1(no. 1):8 (October 1, 1906).

V. RELIGION

1 John Dewey, *A Common Faith* (New Haven: Yale University Press, 1934).
2 Anna Louise Strong, "Some Religious Aspects of Pragmatism," *American Journal of Theology*, 12(no. 2):240 (April 1908). Her Ph.D. dissertation, *The Psychology of Prayer*, was published by the University of Chicago Press in 1909.
3 Edward S. Ames, "Theology from the Standpoint of Functional Psychology," *American Journal of Theology*, 10(no. 2):221 (April 1906).
4 George A. Coe, "Religion from the Standpoint of Functional Psychology," *American Journal of Theology*, 15(no. 2):301–2 (April 1911). Irving King, *The Differentiation of the Religious Consciousness* (New York: Macmillan, 1905); *The Development of Religion* (New York: Macmillan, 1910).
5 Frederick G. Henke, *The Psychology of Ritualism* (Chicago: University of Chicago Press, 1910). Edward S. Ames, *The Psychology of Religious Experience* (Boston: Houghton Mifflin, 1910); reprinted with the same date by Red Label Reprints, New York.
6 Edward S. Ames, "The Psychological Explanation of Religion," *American Journal of Theology*, 15(no. 1):154 (January 1911).
7 Frederick G. Henke, "Advantages Accruing from the Functional View of Religion," *Biblical World*, n.s., 40(no. 6):366–73 (December 1912).
8 *Ibid.*, p. 366.
9 *Ibid.*, p. 367.
10 *Ibid.*, p. 369.
11 *Ibid.*, p. 371.
12 *Ibid.*
13 *Ibid.*, pp. 372–73.
14 Ames, *The Psychology of Religious Experience*, Chapter X.
15 *Ibid.*, p. 318.
16 *Ibid.*, Chapter XII.
17 *Ibid.*, Chapter XI.
18 John Dewey, "Religious Education as Conditioned by Modern Psychology and Pedagogy," in *The Religious Education Association: Proceed-*

ings of the First Annual Convention (Chicago: Executive Office of the Association, 1903), pp. 60–66.

19 Ames, *The Psychology of Religious Experience*, pp. 218–21. Ames refers here to Irving King's *The Psychology of Child Development* (Chicago: University of Chicago Press, 1903).

20 Ames, *The Psychology of Religious Experience*, pp. 250–56.

21 Edward S. Ames, "Theory in Practice," in *Contemporary American Theology: Theological Autobiographies*, Second Series, ed. Vergilius Ferm (New York: Round Table Press, 1933), p. 5.

22 Edward S. Ames, *Religion* (New York: Henry Holt, 1929), pp. 298–99.

23 Edward S. Ames, *Beyond Theology: The Autobiography of Edward Scribner Ames*, ed. Van Meter Ames (Chicago: University of Chicago Press, 1959), p. 76.

24 *Ibid.*, pp. 79–85.

25 See Ames, *The Psychology of Religious Experience*, Chapters VIII and XIV, and *Religion*, Chapter XIV.

26 Quoted in *Beyond Theology*, p. 103, from Ames, *The Divinity of Christ* (Chicago: New Christian Century, 1911).

27 Ames, *Religion*, p. 276.

28 Douglas C. Macintosh, "Pragmatism and Mysticism," *American Journal of Theology*, 15 (no. 1): 142, 143 (January 1911). Macintosh does not criticize Dewey's pragmatism as such, but what he takes to be Dewey's attitude toward religion.

29 John Dewey, "Religion and Our Schools," *Hibbert Journal*, 6 (no. 4): 796–809 (July 1908).

30 John Dewey, "Fundamentals," *New Republic*, 37 (no. 479): 275–76 (February 6, 1924); reprinted in Dewey, *Characters and Events*, ed. Joseph Ratner (2 vols.; New York: Henry Holt, 1929).

31 Dewey, *A Common Faith*, pp. 59–62.

32 Ames, *Religion*, p. 32.

33 Dewey, *A Common Faith*, pp. 9–10.

34 Ames, "Theory in Practice," in *Contemporary American Theology*, pp. 13, 14.

35 Dewey, *A Common Faith*, p. 51.

36 Ames, *Religion*, Chapter X.

37 *Ibid.*, Chapter XI.

38 *Ibid.*, pp. 133–34.

39 Dewey, *A Common Faith*, pp. 43–48.

40 George H. Mead, *The Philosophy of the Act* (Chicago: University of Chicago Press, 1938), p. 475.

41 George H. Mead, "Suggestions toward a Theory of the Philosophical Disciplines," *Philosophical Review*, 9 (no. 1): 17 (January 1900).

42 Mead, *The Philosophy of the Act*, pp. 475–78.

43 George H. Mead, "Scientific Method and the Moral Sciences," *International Journal of Ethics*, 33 (no. 3): 240–44 (April 1923).

44 George H. Mead, *Mind, Self and Society* (Chicago: University of Chicago Press, 1934), pp. 281–98.

45 These papers are in the Archives of the University of Chicago. The first is a typed fragment with pages numbered 18–25. There are two pages numbered 17, three numbered 18, one numbered 19, and one numbered 20 which appear to be different drafts from the eight consecutive pages. The

second paper is a manuscript of thirty-eight consecutive pages, numbered 2–38, of a talk. Neither paper is dated.

46 *Ibid.*, first paper, pp. 19, 20.
47 *Ibid.*, p. 18a.
48 *Ibid.*, p. 20.
49 *Ibid.*, pp. 21–22.
50 *Ibid.*, p. 17b.
51 *Ibid.*, second paper, pp. 37–38.
52 *Ibid.*, pp. 12–13.
53 Mead, "Scientific Method and the Moral Sciences," *International Journal of Ethics*, 33:240.
54 Mead, *Mind, Self and Society*, pp. 296–97.
55 John Dewey and James H. Tufts, *Ethics*, 1st ed. (New York: Henry Holt, 1908), pp. 197–98.
56 James H. Tufts, "On Moral Evolution," *Studies in Philosophy and Psychology*, by Former Students of Charles Edward Garman (Boston: Houghton Mifflin, 1906), p. 39.
57 James H. Tufts, "The Ultimate Test of Religious Truth," *American Journal of Theology*, 14(no. 1):22–24 (January 1910).
58 James H. Tufts, "The Adjustment of the Church to the Psychological Conditions of the Present," *American Journal of Theology*, 12(no. 2):177–82 (April 1908).
59 Dewey, *A Common Faith*, p. 80.
60 See George B. Foster, "Pragmatism and Knowledge," *American Journal of Theology*, 11(no. 4):591–96 (October 1907).
61 James H. Tufts, "George Burman Foster," *University Record (Chicago)*, 5(no. 2):182 (April 1919).
62 George B. Foster, *Christianity in Its Modern Expression* (New York: Macmillan, 1921), pp. 67, 78, 111, 149.
63 Shailer Mathews, "Dean Mathews' Tribute," *University Record (Chicago)*, 18(no. 1):48 (January 1932).
64 Henry N. Wieman, "Intellectual Autobiography," in *The Empirical Theology of Henry Nelson Wieman*, ed. Robert W. Bretall (New York: Macmillan, 1963), pp. 8–10.
65 Winfred E. Garrison, "Transcendental Pluralism," in Ferm, ed., *Contemporary American Theology*, I, 144–45.

VI. SOCIOLOGY, ECONOMICS, AND POLITICAL SCIENCE

1 Howard W. Odum, *American Sociology* (New York: Longmans, Green, 1951), pp. 77–78.
2 *The Demands of Sociology and Pedagogy and My Pedagogic Creed* (New York and Chicago: E. L. Kellogg, 1897).
3 Albion Small and George E. Vincent, *An Introduction to the Study of Society* (New York: American Book, 1894).
4 Albion Small, "The Subject-Matter of Sociology," *American Journal of Sociology*, 10(no. 3):298 (November 1904).
5 Charles R. Henderson, *The Social Spirit in America* (Meadville, Pa.: Flood and Vincent, The Chatauqua-Century Press, 1897).
6 Charles R. Henderson, "Practical Sociology in the Service of Social Ethics," *Investigations Representing the Departments; The Decennial Publi-*

cations of the University of Chicago, First Series, III, Part 1 (Chicago: University of Chicago Press, 1903), pp. 27–49.

7 William I. Thomas, *Source Book for Social Origins* (Chicago: University of Chicago Press, 1909), pp. 16–17. In his comments on the readings in Part II of the book, Thomas says, "The first three selections in Part II may be accepted as sound standpoint for the interpretation of savage mind, and they also contain standpoint for the interpretation of the succeeding parts of the volume" (p. 316). The selections mentioned are Franz Boas, "The Mind of Primitive Man," W. I. Thomas, "The Mind of the Savage," and John Dewey, "Interpretation of Savage Mind."

8 Ernest W. Burgess, "William I. Thomas as a Teacher," *Sociology and Social Research*, 32(no. 2):760 (March–April 1948). See also Harry Elmer Barnes, "William Isaac Thomas: The Fusion of Psychological and Cultural Sociology," in *An Introduction to the History of Sociology*, ed. Barnes (Chicago: University of Chicago Press, 1948), p. 795; and Odum, *American Sociology*, p. 144.

9 Robert E. Park and Ernest W. Burgess, *Introduction to the Science of Sociology* (Chicago: University of Chicago Press, 1921), p. vii.

10 Ellsworth Faris, "The Social Psychology of George Mead," *American Journal of Sociology*, 43(no. 3):393 (November 1937).

11 Ellsworth Faris, Review of *Mind, Self and Society*, *American Journal of Sociology*, 41(no. 6):809, 810 (May 1936).

12 Ellsworth Faris, *The Nature of Human Nature* (New York: McGraw-Hill, 1937), pp. 164–66.

13 Charles A. Ellwood, *Some Prolegomena to Social Psychology* (Chicago: University of Chicago Press, 1910); also in *American Journal of Sociology* as "Prolegomena to Social Psychology," 4(no. 5):656–65 (March 1899); 4(no. 6):807–22 (May 1899); 5(no. 1):98–109 (July 1899); 5(no. 2):220–27 (September 1899).

14 Charles A. Ellwood, *An Introduction to Social Psychology* (New York: D. Appleton, 1917), pp. v–vi.

15 Charles A. Ellwood, "The Sociological Basis of Ethics," *International Journal of Ethics*, 20(no. 3):319, 320 (April 1910).

16 Charles A. Ellwood, *The Psychology of Human Society* (New York: D. Appleton, 1926), pp. vi–vii.

17 Ellwood, "Prolegomena to Social Psychology," *American Journal of Sociology*, 4(no. 6):808, 811 (May 1899); see also Charles A. Ellwood, *Sociology in Its Psychological Aspects* (New York: D. Appleton, 1912), pp. xi, 94, 124, 144; *The Psychology of Human Society*, p. viii. Ellwood makes frequent references to other Chicago figures, including Angell, Ames, Thomas, Henderson, Vincent, Veblen, Loeb, and Irving King.

18 Charles A. Ellwood, *The Reconstruction of Religion: A Sociological View* (New York: Macmillan, 1922), pp. 42, 57, 58, 60, 160.

19 James H. Tufts, Review of *Sociology in Its Psychological Aspects*, *Psychological Bulletin*, 9(no. 12):464–65 (December 15, 1912).

20 Maurice R. Stein, *The Eclipse of Community* (Princeton: Princeton University Press, 1960), p. 324.

21 Thorstein Veblen, *The Theory of the Leisure Class* (New York: Macmillan, 1899).

22 Thorstein Veblen, *The Theory of Business Enterprise* (New York: Charles Scribner's Sons, 1904).

23 Thorstein Veblen, *The Place of Science in Modern Civilisation* (New York: B. W. Huebsch, 1919).
24 Thorstein Veblen, *Essays in Our Changing Order* (New York: Viking Press, 1934).
25 Quoted by Joseph Dorfman in *Thorstein Veblen and His America* (New York: Viking Press, 1934), p. 354.
26 Paul T. Homan, *Contemporary Economic Thought* (New York: Harper and Brothers, 1928), p. 111.
27 Veblen, *The Place of Science in Modern Civilisation*, pp. 74–75.
28 Thorstein Veblen, *Absentee Ownership* (New York: B. W. Huebsch, 1923), p. 16. The reference is to Dewey's *Human Nature and Conduct.*
29 This argument is developed in Veblen's title essay in *The Place of Science in Modern Civilisation*, pp. 1–31; see especially pp. 5–7, 8, 13, 19.
30 Thorstein Veblen, *The Higher Learning in America* (New York: B. W. Huebsch, 1918), p. 27; reissued by Academic Reprints, Stanford, Calif., in 1954.
31 Veblen, *The Place of Science in Modern Civilisation*, p. 5.
32 Dorfman, *Thorstein Veblen and His America*, p. 450.
33 Herbert J. Davenport, "Scope, Method, and Psychology in Economics," *Journal of Philosophy, Psychology, and Scientific Methods*, 14(no. 23): 621, 622 (November 8, 1917).
34 *Ibid.*, p. 618.
35 Wesley C. Mitchell, "Human Behavior and Economics," *Quarterly Journal of Economics*, 29(no. 1):3 (November 1914).
36 Letter from Mitchell to John Maurice Clark dated August 9, 1928. Reproduced in J. M. Clark, *Preface to Social Economics* (New York: Farrar and Rinehart, 1936), pp. 411, 412.
37 Robert F. Hoxie, *Trade Unionism in the United States* (New York: D. Appleton-Century, 1917), p. 57.
38 Clarence E. Ayres, *The Nature of the Relationship between Ethics and Economics* (Chicago: University of Chicago Press, 1918), pp. 20–21.
39 *Ibid.*, pp. 26–29.
40 *Ibid.*, pp. 29–43.
41 *Ibid.*, p. 45.
42 Clarence E. Ayres, *The Theory of Economic Progress* (Chapel Hill: University of North Carolina Press, 1944), p. 220n. See also p. 99 for Ayres's opinion of the relation between Dewey and Veblen.
43 Clarence E. Ayres, *The Divine Right of Capital* (Boston: Houghton Mifflin, 1946), pp. 188–89.
44 Clarence E. Ayres, "Veblen's Theory of Instincts Reconsidered," in *Thorstein Veblen: A Critical Reappraisal*, ed. Douglas F. Dowd (Ithaca, N.Y.: Cornell University Press, 1958), p. 36. Ayres told me a few years ago that he considered himself the only living Deweyite.
45 Henry W. Stuart, "The Hedonistic Interpretation of Subjective Value," *Journal of Political Economy*, 4(no. 1):64–84 (December 1895); "Subjective and Exchange Value," *Journal of Political Economy*, 4(no. 2):208–39 (March 1896); 4(no. 3):352–85 (June 1896).
46 Henry W. Stuart, "Valuation as a Logical Process," in Dewey *et al.*, *Studies in Logical Theory* (Chicago: University of Chicago Press, 1903), pp. 339–40.

47 Charles E. Merriam, *New Aspects of Politics* (Chicago: University of Chicago Press, 1925).

48 See Heinz Eulau, "Political Science," in *A Reader's Guide to the Social Sciences*, ed. Bert F. Hoselitz (Glencoe, Ill.: Free Press, 1959), pp. 91, 107, 124; Leonard D. White, ed., *The State of the Social Sciences* (Chicago: University of Chicago Press, 1956), pp. viii, 334, 348; and Arnold Brecht, *Political Theory* (Princeton: Princeton University Press, 1959), p. 245.

49 Charles E. Merriam, "The Education of Charles E. Merriam," in *The Future of Government in the United States: Essays in Honor of Charles E. Merriam*, ed. Leonard D. White (Chicago: University of Chicago Press, 1942), p. 5.

50 Merriam, *New Aspects of Politics*, pp. xi, xv, 15–18, 40, 165.

51 See especially Harold D. Lasswell, "Psychology and Political Science in the U.S.A.," in *Contemporary Political Science* (Paris: UNESCO, 1950), p. 536.

52 Merriam, "Political Science in the United States," in *Contemporary Political Science*, p. 240.

53 Eulau, "Political Science," in *A Reader's Guide to the Social Sciences*, p. 107.

54 Letter from Harold D. Lasswell to the author, dated February 28, 1968. Other references are to a letter from C. Herman Pritchett, dated February 29, 1968, and one from Quincy Wright, dated March 23, 1968.

55 T. V. Smith, *A Non-Existent Man* (Austin: University of Texas Press, 1962), pp. 45–50.

56 James H. Tufts, "What I Believe," in *Contemporary American Philosophy*, ed. George P. Adams and William Pepperell Montague (New York: Macmillan, 1930), II, 349.

57 Wesley Mitchell, "Research in the Social Sciences," in *The New Social Science*, ed. Leonard D. White (Chicago: University of Chicago Press, 1930), pp. 10–11.

VII. AFTERWORD

1 John Dewey, *Experience and Nature* (La Salle, Ill.: Open Court, 1958), p. 241.

Index

INDEX

INDEX

INDEX

Index

INDEX